Congratulations!

You've Been Fired

Congratulations!

You've Been Fired

Sound Advice for Women Who've Been Terminated Pink-Slipped Downsized or Otherwise Unemployed

EMILY KOLTNOW
and Lynne S. Dumas

FAWCETT COLUMBINE · NEW YORK

A Fawcett Columbine Book
Published by Ballantine Books
Copyright © 1990 by Emily Koltnow and Lynne S. Dumas

Library of Congress Catalog Card Number: 89-92593

ISBN: 0-449-90443-1

Cover design by William Geller
Cover photograph © 1990 Anthony Loew
Interior design by Ann Gold
Manufactured in the United States of America
First Edition: September 1990
10 9 8 7 6 5 4 3

To my husband and best pal,
Larry—what a guy!
To the memory of my dad, Bill Numeroff,
and to my mom, Florence,
both of whom taught me the joy of living.
                              —E.K.

To my husband, Dominick Scotto, for his warmth and wit,
counsel and confidence,
and to Bear, for everything else.
                              —L.D.

CONTENTS

AUTHORS' NOTE

This book is a collaboration between its two coauthors: "unemployment specialist" Emily Koltnow and writer Lynne S. Dumas. But because much of the information is based on Emily's WIN Workshops, and we wanted to capture as much of the flavor and feeling of the workshop sessions as possible, we chose to write our book in Emily's voice.

Also, for reasons of confidentiality, firees who wanted their names withheld have been given pseudonyms.

ACKNOWLEDGMENTS

The pages of this book represent the help and support of so many people, it's difficult to know where to begin. But if it were not for Carole Hyatt, who godmothered this project, our collaborative effort might never have occurred. Thanks, Carole.

Our appreciation also goes to our agent, Lynn Seligman, for believing in this project from Day One and for providing many insights into the publishing world; to our editor, Betsy Rapoport, for her enthusiasm, perceptive suggestions, and guidance; and to Joelle Delbourgo, for recognizing a great idea when she saw one.

We'd also like to extend our thanks to the professional experts who gave of themselves so willingly: Leslie Rose, Dr. Marilyn Puder-York, Jane Ames, Linda Eidelberg, Eric J. Wallach, Madeleine Swain, Andrew Cooper, Dr. Kenneth Frank, Dr. Tessa Albert Warschaw, Gloria Waslyn, Mary Ann Lee, Jim Brady, Ellen Flamholtz, Bill Morin, Herman Bott, Maureen Hunt, Kathy Conners, Joan Bowman, Jeannette Scollard, Jane Antil, Dr. Barrie S. Greiff, and Ann Hunt, Marcia Gillespie, Carolyn Gottfried, Harriet Michel, Joseph De-Gennaro, and Bernadette Mansur.

Special thanks to Julie Lewit-Nirenberg, Linda Ellerbee, Sally Jessy Raphael, Bobbi Van, Ruth Kintzer, Laura Baldosare, Anna Riback-Gibson, Suzanne Kiefer, Anne Luther, Pat Brownstone, Nancy Smith, and the hundreds of WIN Workshop participants and survey respondents who so generously shared their own stories.

Lynne's personal thank-you to Edith and Marcel Dumas for their encouragement and support. And Emily's appreciation to Joan Terranova, Lenore Benson, Wendy D'Amico, Rhoda, Muffy, Lee, Andrea, Sherry, Terri, Michelle, Suzi, Jeanne, Penny, Silvi, Arlene, Amy, Pat, Suzanne, Esther, Roslyn, E.M., and Renee for helping lay the foundation for WIN Workshops.

And finally, from us both, thanks to Sandy Kaye, Irving Rousso, Howard Sacharoff, Laura Pomerantz, and Herschel Cravitz for having fired Emily and given this book its start.

Congratulations!

You've Been Fired

1.

Congratulations! You've Been Fired

So you've been fired. Congratulations!

Bet no one's said that to you yet. More than likely, you've been hearing from well-meaning friends and loved ones comments like "Oh, I'm sorry to hear that," or "You must feel horrible! How terribly unfair!" or even "I can't believe this could have happened to you! You were so good at your job."

These condolences, delivered with the best of intentions, may be comforting. But truth be told, they're not very helpful. Because what they do best is fuel your self-pity, anxiety about the future, and anger at your company. Not that these emotions aren't understandable, justifiable, and very, very real. Of course they are. But it's counterproductive to let them control you.

Look. I know how bad you feel. Over the course of my career, I've been fired more than once! And each time, I felt just like you do now—rotten. Also angry, scared, depressed, anxious, and worried that I'd never work again. But let me tell you something: Getting fired was the best thing that ever happened to me, just as it was for the hundreds of other professional women I've worked with over the last few years, some of whom you'll meet in this book. And here's even better news: As unlikely as it seems right now, getting fired can be a wonderful opportunity for you, too.

Losing your job opens your options and offers a second chance to place yourself in a career situation that's exciting, challenging—even fun!

Hard to believe? Look at it this way. Chances are that when you began your particular career path, you hit the ground running and haven't stopped since. But now that you've been pink-slipped, you can stop and catch your breath, look around at where you've been, how far you've come, and, most important, where you're going.

Getting fired gives you a long-overdue opportunity to reassess your likes and dislikes, reevaluate your priorities, and redirect your energies to achieve the position or career you really want. I'm not just talking about stopping to smell the roses here; I'm talking about planting a few new ones, too.

Let me quote a great philosopher—my mother. She always told me that despite initial appearances, things happen for the best. I'm convinced that when it comes to being fired, that's absolutely true.

The first time I was fired, I found a new job at twice the salary; the last time, I started my own business. With just about each firing in between, I landed better jobs at better companies. Today, I'm the most successful I've ever been. I created and now run my own business, WIN Workshops, in which I'm a catalyst in other women's careers. I'm a frequent guest on TV talk shows, have been featured in publications ranging from *Cosmopolitan* to *Business Week*, and often speak to women's groups across the country. And now, I'm even an author. And the same terrific things can happen for you.

Still doubtful? Just stop for a moment and think about your last job. Then answer these questions. Be honest, now.

- Which did you look forward to more, Monday morning or Friday afternoon?
- Did you frequently avoid certain parts of your job, putting them off as long as possible, or did you tackle every task enthusiastically?

4

- Were you underpaid or well-compensated?
- Were you underappreciated or highly valued?
- Were you so comfortable with your job that you were just coasting, or were you genuinely challenged?
- Was your boss a pain-in-the-neck or a generous mentor?
- Had you topped out in your company, or was there room for advancement?

If any of your answers made you anxious or uneasy—and I'll bet that at least one of them did—then maybe getting fired wasn't such a great loss after all. Even if this exercise reinforced the fact that you absolutely loved the job you lost, I contend you can still find a new one that's more interesting, more satisfying, and maybe even better paying.

Take it from Julie Lewit-Nirenberg, publisher of *Mirabella*. Today, she's working on this new and exciting magazine, making good money, and loving what she does. But several years ago, her future seemed a lot more bleak.

"I was the advertising director at *Savvy* magazine and doing quite well. But the Wednesday before the July Fourth weekend, the publisher called me into his office and said he had to make some changes; he was letting me go. No notice, no warnings—I was in a state of shock. I mean, I had helped launch that publication!

"Well, I barely made it out of his office. I had never been fired before! Then, I started to cry. I felt like someone had kicked me in the stomach; I actually felt physically sick. After the initial shock wore off, I thought, 'What did I do wrong?' I felt inadequate and that I must be a terrible person. I worried if I would ever get a job again—and if I did, what kind of job could it be?"

Nonetheless, Julie gathered up her sagging self-esteem and started interviewing. "I remember telling people that I'd been fired and being surprised at their reaction; all they said was, 'Well, everybody good gets fired at least once in their lives'!"

It didn't take Julie long to land another job—for more money, incidentally—as the group advertising director for *Esquire* magazine. "As it turned out, getting fired was the best thing that ever happened to me. I learned a huge amount at *Esquire*." Later, Julie launched *New York Woman* as publisher and eventually accepted her current position at *Mirabella*.

"It's all been great, and one of the best things that happened was that several years after I'd been fired I ran into the man who fired me. He told me that letting me go was the worst mistake he'd ever made! Talk about satisfaction!"

What I love most about Julie's story is that, happily, it's not that unusual. Many, if not most, managerial women are able to place themselves into better, more gratifying positions even when their pink slip is showing.

Here's my message: Yes, getting fired hurts. But it also helps, because it acts as a powerful catalyst that moves you closer to realizing your unique potential. And, if you follow the chapter-by-chapter advice in this book, advice that has worked for hundreds of women who also lost their jobs, you can turn what you now believe is a liability into a personal and professional asset. So . . . Congratulations!

My Own Story

At 11:30 A.M. on Thursday, January 8, 1987, I was earning over $100,000 a year as vice president of merchandising for Smith & Jones, a women's clothing manufacturer. By 11:35 A.M., I was unemployed.

It wasn't the first time in my twenty-three-year career that I'd been fired; that kind of thing happens all the time in the fashion industry. But it was the worst. And it hurt the most.

As a vice president, I had felt invulnerable. After all, I had an impressive title, respect in my field, and authority in supervising an entire division. I had an office with a spectacular view of the Hudson River, two European business trips a year, a personal annual expense account. Certainly, I was immune to being fired at this high level.

Wrong!

That day, my boss came to me and said, "We're going to have to make a lot of changes in your department." As a good employee, I immediately started calculating how I could cut back and still run an effective design room. Then I heard his next sentence: "And we're starting with you."

There, he had said it. In fact, he had planned to say it for quite a while, but I just hadn't seen it coming.

Of course, I was shocked. Surprisingly, though, I was also relieved. To be honest, I had been dissatisfied with my job for about a year but was too complacent to do anything about it. My salary, which I knew I couldn't replace easily, also kept me from taking action.

But now I'd been fired. Once my boss, now my ex-boss, left my office, I called my husband, who couldn't have been more supportive. Then I went outside to face my staff. They all knew already—I could tell by their expressions. For a moment, we just stared at each other; then we all hugged and cried.

On the train home that night, I felt jealous of everyone, from the ticket taker to the conductor. After all, they were working and I wasn't. I was a failure. Somehow, I had never realized before how much I had allowed my sense of self to be defined by my work.

I'd never kept a diary, but going home that night I took out a little notebook and wrote:

"I feel somewhat relieved, but also a major sense of loss. It's kind of like a divorce, because the company was like my family. And even if you know it's not your fault, you still feel pretty crummy. It's belittling to have to call people and explain. Then, when the receptionist asks, 'What company are you with?' you have to say 'Nowhere.'

"I MUST write a résumé."

I've always been a great sleeper, but that night I awoke at 3:00 A.M. filled with anxiety. I worried: "Who will ever hire me again? I was so lucky to have had this job for five years; but I had them fooled. Now they've discovered that I was a fraud. How will I ever prove myself? Will I ever get another job?"

With the break of day, and with my adrenaline pumping, I began my job search. But days became weeks became months, and nothing panned out. A few awful interviews were the closest I came to anything that even sniffed of employment.

Somehow, I forced myself to attend the monthly meeting of Fashion Group, a professional women's association. There, I happened to sit next to Wendy, the vice president of creative services for a major cosmetics firm. As we listened to the speaker, my friend Joan leaned over to me and said, "Do you know that you and Wendy are in the same boat?" I turned to Wendy and whispered, "You were fired, too?" She nodded.

After the meeting, Wendy and I started talking—and talking and talking and talking. She had just been fired and was devastated. Though I was hurting, she seemed in even worse shape (after all, this was only her first firing in twenty-five years of steady work), and I felt I could help her. We formed an instant bond. I related all the things she could expect to feel—anxiety, inadequacy, a sense of failure, that it was all her fault, that no one would hire her again. She smiled; I had touched a nerve. When I confessed that Monday mornings, when everyone else went off to work, made me feel the worst, and that I looked forward to Friday afternoons, not because they were the start of the weekend but because no one else was working either, she laughed despite herself.

Over the next few weeks we started to meet for lunch, for brunch, for tea; after all, we were "ladies of leisure." During that time, four other women we knew were also fired, so I arranged for the six of us to meet.

We got together at a Japanese restaurant where three notable things happened: (1) no one checked her coat (because it would cost a dollar to retrieve it), (2) no one ordered a drink (gone were those expense account lunches—even Perrier costs), and (3) no one could stop talking. One woman, a former corporate executive, didn't even order lunch, insisting that she had had a huge breakfast. It wasn't until six months later that she could comfortably confess she'd been too scared to spend any money on such an indulgence as a restaurant lunch.

We exchanged stories about the interviews we were or were not having, shared our anxieties, and laughed, albeit bittersweetly, through it all. When it was over, we agreed this was the best we'd felt in a long time and decided to meet again.

The very next day, I called Lenore Benson, the executive director of The Fashion Group Intl., and enlisted her cooperation in asking other members if they would be interested in joining our luncheon group. I typed up a brief questionnaire about being fired, distributed it to the membership, and almost immediately got twenty responses. Within two weeks, an informal support group began meeting regularly.

Our first session brought a catharsis for us all. After exchanging résumés, each woman told her personal firing story. Words like "frightened," "lost," "panicked," "out of control," and "bag lady" peppered these talks. One common theme—concern about finances—emerged over and over again. Even though these were bright, professionally successful women, many were single or divorced and had to pay hefty rents and mortgages. One woman was putting her sons through medical school on her own. Even those of us who were married and living in two-income families were worried.

After all, our incomes, like the incomes of most women today, were not frivolous ones used for vacations and spending sprees. They paid for rent, groceries, insurance. And after you've been earning a respectable salary, as all of us were, unemployment benefits just don't cut it, especially because none of us had any idea how long it would be before we'd be working again.

These meetings, which continued for weeks, were not only comforting but informative as well. I started arranging for guest speakers, including a career counselor, a lawyer, a psychologist, an executive recruiter, even an image consultant. Soon, the job I'd lost in the apparel industry seemed farther and farther away. I began to realize that although seminars and workshops were available for just about every facet of working—from stress management to assertiveness training to how to be a better boss—none existed to help women when they needed it most, when they felt most alone; that is, when they were fired.

Gradually, my direction became clear. I would take my support group and turn it into a business: running educational, support, and networking groups for women who had lost their jobs. WIN Workshops was born.

First Things First: WINbreakers

Now that you've heard my story, let's concentrate on yours. There's lots to do after you get fired. And lots to know, as you'll discover in this book. But don't panic; we'll get it all done. For now, just put first things first. It's called prioritizing, something you'll be doing a lot of throughout this whole process. So let's get started.

What you need to begin with are WINbreakers; like icebreakers, they help you get going. Begin today—all right, maybe tomorrow—but don't wait too long. They're too important. These twelve steps will help you take concrete action toward beginning your new job search with confidence.

(1) REGISTER FOR UNEMPLOYMENT

Guess what? In most states (though not all, so check your own), you are entitled to collect unemployment concurrently with any severance you may be getting. It surprises me how few women know that.

But what amazes me even more is that many women are embarrassed to register for unemployment at all. They feel humiliated getting on a line, in public, and admitting that they're out of work. Let's get something straight right away: There's absolutely no reason to feel that way.

First of all, unemployment compensation is money that you and your employer have been contributing out of your paycheck on a regular basis while you were working, so it's money to which you are legitimately entitled. Second, in some states today you no longer have to stand on line each week to get your check; once you register, you'll receive your compensation by mail. And third, if and when you do have to wait on line, it gives you an opportunity to network. You'd be surprised how many top-notch professionals are lining up these days. You're there, aren't you?

The amount of money you can expect to take home from unemployment benefits—and the duration of coverage—is state regulated, so contact your local unemployment office to find out what you'll receive. It may not seem like much on a weekly basis—for example, to date the maximum you can collect in New York State is $245 a week—but if you're out of work for ten weeks, that's $2,450 and nothing to sneeze at.

Or perhaps what happened to me might happen to you. While I was looking for a new position and going on interviews, I was developing the concept for WIN Workshops. By the time my six months of unemployment benefits had elapsed, my business had crystalized and WIN was on its way. Had I not registered for unemployment, I would have missed out on several thousands of dollars that paid some bills and subsidized the launch of my new venture.

Ready to sign up? Great. And since it can take several weeks to process the paperwork and get your first check, register NOW.

(2) GET YOURSELF A PERSONAL BUSINESS CARD

It's unprofessional to take your old business card, scratch out the now-useless office number, and write in your home phone. And having no card to hand out at all is even worse.

What happens if you bump into an old college friend, former colleague, or other potential contact on the street and after chatting, she (or he) says, "Where can I get in touch with you?" You launch into a circus act, juggling a handbag, packages, and umbrella while you search for a pen. Then you jot down the information on the first piece of paper you find, probably an old, crumpled receipt, hand it to her, and hope that she doesn't lose it. Even if she finds it six months later, it will be too late to do you any good.

Don't let that happen to you. Instead, call a few printers and shop around for the best price on a new business card with your name, address, and home phone and/or answering service number. The cost will vary greatly depending upon what part of the country you're in and how fancy a style you choose. Usually, though, you can get several hundred printed for less than $50, and they're more than worth the price. Even if you're lucky enough to land a new position quickly, they're not a total loss—they make great social cards.

Personal business cards will also help you feel a whole lot more professional when someone asks for your number. For a few ideas on card styles and designs, see the examples opposite.

(By the way, matching your cards to your résumés makes a more professional impression when you do a mailing, so take that into consideration before having either printed.)

(3) CONSIDER A GENERIC BUSINESS CARD

If you are clearly focused on what your next professional move will be, add to your name, address, and phone a generic description of what it is you do when you get your business cards printed. For example, "landscape architect," "systems analyst," "special events coordinator" or "food stylist" tells someone a little more about yourself and conveys the idea that you know what you want and are committed to it. If you want to do any free-lancing or consulting while you're searching for a full-time position, these cards will serve you well. Such cards can also help you get into trade shows where business cards are often requested upon registration. (More on the importance of trade shows in another chapter.)

(4) SECURE A LIBRARY CARD

I'm embarrassed to admit that I didn't have a library card when I got fired. I wasn't even aware of what the library offered me. Although bookstores are rich sources of publications that you absolutely must own—you know, those you want to write in, highlight, dog-ear, and make a permanent part of your personal library (like this one, of course)—libraries also offer a wealth of job-search-related materials. You'll find books on any career you might want to explore, from advertising to zoology. Out-of-print or hard-to-find books, magazine and newspaper articles, annual reports, pamphlets, even records and videotapes are also accessible at most decent-sized libraries.

I speak from experience. When I was fired and started my support group, I needed to research how people cope with being out of work. I went to the library and learned to use the computer. The first question it asked me was "subject requested." I punched in "F-I-R-E-D"

Jane Gilman
87 N.E. 34th Avenue
Miami, FL 33054
(305) 555-2033

Brenda DeLuca

3 WEST 12th St. N.Y.C.N.Y.10011·555-2962

Patricia Handler
2 TURTLE CREEK BLVD.
DALLAS, TX 75219
—
(214)555-2212

SHARON BIRNBAUM

2 sunset hill rd. redding, ct 06896
(203) 555-0491

ANNA MARIE AMERUSO

18 EAST 87th STREET NYC 10028 212-555-8187

NANCY ARNOLD
120 ROCK HILL ROAD
BALA CYNWYD, PA 19004
215-555-2240

HANNAH STONE
6 OLDE IVY SQUARE
ATLANTA, GA 30342
(404) 555-8481

Pamela Carter

49 Sohap Land, Columbia, MD 21045
(301) 555-1572

CAROLE ROSS
ADVERTISING CONSULTANT

(617) 555-1944   (617) 555-6725

Priscilla Markell
Publisher
80 Lincoln Drive
Phoenix, AZ 85018
—
(602) 555-1172

and eagerly awaited a deluge of data. What popped up on the screen were articles and books on "Fire Engines." Close but no cigar. Then I tried "Business," then "Women and Business," and I was home free.

While surprisingly little existed on getting fired (which is why we're writing this book), there were enough magazine articles to get me started. The library was like one-stop shopping. All the back issues were in binders and I was able to read fifty articles and photocopy those I wanted to keep for further reference.

Libraries give you a tremendous amount of job-search materials, all organized under one roof. Make friends with your library now; it will save you lots of time later.

(5) GET YOUR TERMINATION STORY STRAIGHT

Very often, the last thing you want to know when you've just been fired is precisely why. But that's exactly what prospective employers will ask during an interview. It's also what they'll ask your former boss when they do a reference check. And believe me, if they do a check with only one person, it will be your ex-employer, not someone from that list of glowing references you've provided.

So get your story straight. As difficult as it is, take a deep breath and call your ex-boss—or, in some large companies, the personnel or human resource director—and discuss what you both can say comfortably when anyone asks.

By the way, don't use "I resigned" as a good termination story if you've been fired. It's neither true nor honest, and no savvy potential employer will buy it. A much better idea is to agree with your ex-boss on something like "The company was going in a new direction and no longer needed my particular expertise," or "New management decided to bring in its own team."

Once you reach an agreement, request a letter of reference; it's the perfect time to ask for one if you haven't done so already. Presenting this letter to potential employers might even forestall their calling your former boss.

If your ex-employer won't take your calls or if you left on such a sour note that you really don't want to speak with him or her at all, then you need the next WINbreaker.

(6) CHECK UP ON YOUR REFERENCE

Find someone, perhaps a former supplier or a friendly colleague, who could reasonably pretend to be interviewing you for the type of position you are seeking, and have this person call your ex-employer for a reference. That way, you can learn what is being said about you.

Don't think it's important? Listen to this. When Irene was fired, her boss said, "Feel free to use me as a reference." Luckily, before she did, she took my advice and had a friend check it out. Sure enough, when the ex-boss was asked if she would recommend Irene, she replied, "I don't know you, but I wouldn't do that to you." When Irene heard that, it hurt, but she knew it was better that her friend, rather than a possible employer, had gotten that response. Now Irene had the information she needed to prevent this from happening with a *real* potential boss.

What Irene did was to rewrite her "interview script." That is, when people asked if they could call her former boss for a reference, she simply said, "By all means, call. However, understand that she and I had very different work styles. I am a self-starter, which made her uncomfortable and is probably the main reason we parted ways. So let me also give you some other people to call in that company who were familiar with the quality of my work."

Then, even when these reference seekers phoned the ex-boss and got a negative response, they were prepared, so the comments did not have much impact. What's more, these potential bosses also called the other references, who offered nothing but accolades. (FYI: Irene landed a new job within one month after her firing, despite the grudging attitude of her previous employer.)

(7) GET YOUR RÉSUMÉ UNDER WAY

Since résumés are so important, I'm going to devote chapter 6 to them. But you need to do a few things immediately to get the process going.

First, pull out your old résumé. If it's up to date and powerful, you're one step ahead. But if you're like most of us and either don't have a résumé or have an outdated or unimpressive one, then start collecting as many as you can from other professional women in your field.

The reason is simple. Have you ever hired anyone to work for you? If so, you've had the opportunity to see lots of résumés from subordinates. But how often have you gotten to hire a peer? Rarely, is my guess. This is unfortunate, since very often during a job search you will be judged by how well (or poorly) your résumé stacks up against those of your peers. So gather up at least half a dozen samples through professional organizations, friends, and colleagues. You'll be amazed at how quickly they can help you reevaluate and improve your own.

When you're ready to write your résumé, I recommend you use a word processor or home computer, or find a firm that offers such services. If word processing isn't available to you, or you choose not to use it, then you need to shop around for a printer. Find one that will give you the best price for the quality of résumé you want. And don't forget to ask how long it will take to get them. Overnight is great but may cost you more; two weeks is too long to wait. A good way to get a lead on some effective printers is to ask the people whose résumés you really like.

One more point to consider: If you already have a fabulous résumé, you may be tempted to start sending it out to executive recruiters. That's okay, but don't expect to get much of a response. Misconceptions about headhunters abound, and one of the most common is that it's their job to find you a job. Not true. An executive recruiter is hired by a company to find a qualified candidate to fill a specific position.

Recruiters work for the employer, not the employee, so they

probably won't be able to spend any time discussing your career goals or plotting a job-search strategy with you. But don't worry. They'll get in touch with you when and if your qualifications fit their needs. (For more on executive recruiters and how they can help, see chapter 6. But not yet. It's important for you to take things step by step. Trust me; we'll cover everything in time!)

(8) MAKE SURE YOUR COBRA IS IN PLACE

If you were covered by a company insurance plan, the Consolidated Omnibus Reconciliation Act of 1985 (COBRA) is something you should know about. In broad strokes, it allows you the option of purchasing continued health insurance coverage after you've been terminated. In most cases, you and your dependents will be eligible to continue insurance for up to eighteen months, provided you were not fired for gross misconduct.

If you worked for a company with fewer than twenty employees (including parent and subsidiaries), or are covered by Medicare or another medical insurance plan, you probably won't have these rights extended to you, but do check with the human resource person at your firm to be sure. Another exception: If you work for a federal agency, you're also not protected by COBRA. But a recently enacted law gives similar rights to federal employees. For more information, write to the Office of Personnel Management in Washington, D.C.

If you are protected by COBRA, and most of you are, here's how it works. First, your company will notify you of your COBRA rights; if by some chance it doesn't, ask. Then, you'll have about sixty days to exercise your option to pay for continued coverage. Once you choose this option, you will be responsible for the amount the company pays to have its active employees insured, plus another 2 percent to cover administrative costs. For instance, if you and your company have each been paying $50 a month for your medical insurance, you will now have to pay $100 plus 2 percent, or a total of $102 each month for the same coverage as a working employee. I know this seems like a lot to pay at a time when money is a concern, but believe me, it's a whole lot less expensive than buying an individual policy—and you can't afford to be without insurance.

What I've just outlined is COBRA in a nutshell. As is the case with most government regulations, though, there are several twists and turns that make it a little tricky to understand. For more specific information, check with your firm's personnel department, or write to the U.S. Department of Labor, Pension and Welfare Benefits Administration, Office of Program Services, Division of Technical Assistance & Inquiry, Room N 5658, 200 Constitution Avenue NW, Washington, D.C. 20210.

(9) RETAIN A LAWYER?

I've put a question mark here because as angry as you might be and as unfairly as you may have been treated, suing your former employer may not be your best move. First of all, wrongful discharge suits, as they're called in the trade, are tough to win. Most states have "at-will" laws, which means that an employer can terminate an employee for almost any reason or for no reason at all; that is, they can fire you "at will," no matter how unjust you believe the reason to be. The only exception is losing your job because of discrimination according to race, religion, national origin, age, sex, or physical disability.

Second, even if you don't live in a pure "at-will" state, court cases are lengthy and costly. I know of one woman who sued her employer and, three years after the final ruling, is still paying off her legal debts. (Adding insult to injury, she lost the case.)

Eric Wallach, a prominent New York attorney who specializes in employment practices and employment practices litigation, offers this point of view: "So many of these lawsuits are wasteful exercises. They take a long time—can go on for years—and serve to paralyze your ability to get on with your life.

"Remember, too, that it takes two to tango. While you may be very angry, if you sue, your company often gets just as angry and emotional. Typically, its reaction is, 'This is an outrage! We have treated this person well for many years, and we'll fight this.' Ultimately, because of all the aggravation and expense involved, these cases usually get settled out of court."

What's more, it's been Wallach's experience that such settlements are small—employees often win no more than three months' salary. Thus, he says, "It's my opinion that in most cases you'd be better off not suing and using your time and energy calmly trying to negotiate a good severance and find a new job."

In some situations, however, a lawsuit is warranted. For instance, if you've been fired because of discrimination on the basis of sex, race, age, or physical handicap, you may well have good, solid grounds. What constitutes such grounds? That depends upon the particular case. But just as an example, let's say you believe you were fired because you're a woman. According to Wallach, there are three ways to prove sex discrimination.

(1) DIRECT EVIDENCE: In a one-on-one firing, the best proof is specific, concrete facts. For instance, you would have powerful evidence if a person in authority made a derogatory statement to you regarding your sex (e.g., "I can't trust a woman to do that"), or if you were flatly excluded from meetings because they were held at clubs or outings from which women were barred.

(2) STATISTICAL EVIDENCE: This pertains more to downsizing or massive layoffs than it does to one-on-one firings. In a large company, you may be able to demonstrate that women were disproportionately laid off in a downsizing. For instance, if 10 percent of the staff were let go and 75 percent of those laid off were women, you might have persuasive grounds for a case.

(3) CIRCUMSTANTIAL EVIDENCE: Since statistical evidence doesn't work in a small department, you may be able to prove your case with circumstantial evidence. If, for example, four or five people discharged in a ten-person department were women, you might have a solid basis for a lawsuit.

If you feel that you might have legitimate grounds to take your former employer to court, or if you had a written employment contract that you believe was violated, by all means consult an attorney, preferably one who specializes in labor and employment practices. Sometimes, even if you don't have a strong enough case to win a lawsuit, a lawyer can prove helpful in negotiating a good severance package. (I've helped lots of women do this themselves, though, as you'll discover in chapter 4.) To find a good attorney, ask friends and colleagues for referrals or call your state Bar Association.

One important tip: Come prepared for your legal consultation. Bring copies of your contract, any reviews, evaluations, termination letter—any and all information that could help document your case.

Before we leave the legal question once and for all, I want to address a fear that many people have when deciding whether or not to sue their company: being blackballed. I wish I could reassure you that this doesn't happen, but unfortunately it does, especially if you're involved in a small, tightly woven industry where everyone knows everyone else. Being blackballed is a risk that you must weigh against what you hope to gain, whether that is money, self-respect, justice, or just plain revenge.

If you are blackballed (and that's an "if," not a "when"), you're going to have to deal with it. While it may be disheartening, it's not impossible to get around. Again, if you treat it as an opportunity for change, a time to reexamine what it is you can do and where you can do it, you'll be back on your feet soon, hopefully in an industry that's better suited to your particular talents and strengths.

(10) SET UP YOUR WORKPLACE

The ideal situation is if your former company gives you individual outplacement, i.e., job-search assistance provided to former employees upon termination (and usually exclusive to senior management). One of the key benefits is that the outplacement firm supplies you with an office and all of its services—secretary, receptionist, photocopier, and so on. Then you're all set. But that's an unlikely scenario for most women.

The next best thing is to find a workplace outside your home, perhaps at a friend's or relative's company, where you'll have your own desk and use of a phone. (Make sure that phone number is listed on your new business card.) This will get you up, dressed, and out every day, put you in a professional atmosphere with other working people, and add structure to your daily routine. If you can afford it, you may want to consider renting office space.

If none of these options is available to you, though, you are going to have to launch your job search out of your home. This has obvious negatives—you'll be tempted to sleep late or turn on the TV, or you could be distracted by pets, kids, your husband, or neighbors who think you're available to coffee klatch. To counteract this, create an official home office. It can be a corner of a studio apartment, your former guest room—any place that's hands-off to anyone but you.

Set up your workplace with your telephone, pencils, pens, notepads, stationery, envelopes, résumés, business cards, Scotch tape, staples, paper clips, correction fluid, stamps (you'll need plenty of these), and folders. A typewriter, home computer, or word processor and a small filing cabinet are also good investments, or you can rent them by the month. Remember, you can't go down the hall to the supply room anymore, so prepare yourself.

(11) BUY AN ANSWERING MACHINE

With the exception of a résumé, an answering machine is the most indispensable tool for the unemployed. Once you start your job-hunting campaign, it will keep you from missing important callbacks. Additionally, when you receive a message from an important contact, you have the opportunity to call back and say, "This is Emily Koltnow, _returning_ Mr. Turner's call," which increases the likelihood that you'll get past the secretary and through to Mr. Turner.

If you shop around, you can find a reliable machine for under $100. Just make sure you get one that allows you to call in from outside phones for messages, too, so that you don't always have to be near the machine to find out who called. Don't forget to list the number of your answering machine on your business card if it's a separate line.

Use your answering machine professionally. If you're married or have a roommate, make sure your voice is the only one on the recorded message. For as long as it takes you to find another position, your phone message should sound as professional as possible. This means no music in the background, no cutesy messages, and no Mae West impressions, please!

Be sure to include your name, not just your number, on the outgoing message. Many of the people who will be calling won't be familiar with your voice and won't be certain they've reached you until they hear your name. Also, when potential employers or valuable contacts call you from a busy office, they may get distracted and forget who they dialed. Hearing your name, not just your number, will remind them.

(12) LOCATE HELPFUL ORGANIZATIONS

There are lots of organizations scattered across the United States that can prove extremely useful to you; I'll talk more about this in chapter 7. But for now, get hold of the *Encyclopedia of Associations* (it's available in most good-sized libraries) and look up those associations appropriate for (1) working women in general and (2) your industry in particular. For instance, NAFE (National Association of Female Executives), an organization with local groups in every state, is listed and you may find it a good, broad-based group to contact. Or, if you're interested in journalism, you'll find the American Society of Journalists and Authors, an excellent resource for editors, writers, agents, and publishers.

Many states and cities also have individualized directories worth probing. Just ask your librarian for guides that will work for you.

These WINbreakers will not only get you moving in the right direction but also give you a revitalizing sense of control over your professional life. So, congratulations! Your newest job—finding that next great job—has just begun.

2.

It's 9:00 A.M. Do You Know Where Your Job Is?

You breeze into the office early Monday morning, ready to tackle another week. You pour yourself a cup of coffee, peruse your messages, and check out your appointment book for the day's schedule. Suddenly, the boss's secretary calls: "Mr. Kramer would like to see you in his office."

You glance at the clock—9:00 A.M.—and wonder: "We usually don't meet until lunch. Why does he want to see me now?" You feel a stab of anxiety, but it passes quickly. "Oh, well," you think, "it couldn't be anything important." But guess what? It may well be time to clean out your desk.

In researching this book, my collaborator, Lynne, and I sent a questionnaire to hundreds of just-fired women around the country. Our survey uncovered these interesting facts about firings:

• Most people get fired on Monday morning, or, if Monday was a holiday, on Tuesday morning. Fully 40 percent of all respondents got the ax during one of those two times.

• The next most popular time to get fired is Friday. But if you're terminated on that day, it won't be until late in the afternoon, probably near closing. Our survey revealed that 30 percent of respondents got fired on Friday afternoon.

(By the way, our findings jibe with information provided by top executives and human resource professionals. When it comes to letting someone go, they fall into one of two camps: Monday morning or Friday afternoon firers. The former believe that firing early in the week gives ex-employees the opportunity to contact the unemployment office and get right to work job hunting. Friday firers hold that their first responsibility is to the remaining staff; they believe getting ex-staffers out fast, without the opportunity to return the next day, has the least disruptive, demoralizing effect on those still working. Also, they feel it lets firees calm down and collect their thoughts over the weekend and begin the work week, now their job-hunting week, anew.)

• The least common time slot in which people get fired is noon to 2:00 P.M. So if your boss invites you to lunch, relax. It's probably business as usual.

• Getting your walking papers doesn't take long. It took only five to fifteen minutes for 77 percent of our respondents to be told they no longer had a job, whether they had worked at their company for six months or sixteen years!

• Some 47 percent of our respondents admit they saw warning signs but chose to ignore them. To return to our original scenario, being summoned to your boss's office first thing Monday is probably not a good sign, but that's especially true if it makes you anxious. Most likely, your anxiety signals that you *knew* something was wrong, but just hadn't bothered to face it before.

I call it "corporate graffiti"—the handwriting on the office wall—and I'll discuss it in detail in a later chapter. But for now, suffice it to say that if you feel like kicking yourself for not having paid attention to the warning signs that in retrospect seem blatant, you're in good company.

Why We Get Fired

If you're like the hundreds of recent firees I've spoken with, you're convinced your firing was unique. And in a sense it was, because it happened to you under a particular set of circumstances and you reacted to it in your own individual way. But chances are the reason you were discharged was a relatively common one. In fact, our research reveals that in most cases we get fired for one of four main reasons:

(1) New management;
(2) Office politics;
(3) Economics; and
(4) Personality conflicts.

Why haven't I listed poor performance? Don't most people get bounced because they're not doing their job well?

No. Actually, only a very small percentage of people—I've heard figures ranging from 5 to 15 percent—lose their jobs because they're not working up to par.

That being the case, then, let's take a closer look at each of those four major causes of job loss:

(1) NEW MANAGEMENT

Many of you, regardless of your current state of unemployment, have at some time or another held a new position in which you supervised others. When you were hired for that job, your boss probably advised you not to make any changes right away. Even if you were told to cut or expand staff, you were urged to wait until you could evaluate your needs.

Well, the basic strategy didn't change just because you were on the flip side of such new-management maneuvering. Rest assured that your new boss was told the same thing you were in the same circumstance—so, if you were smart, you realized the ax could fall.

Losing your job because of new management has become much more common today, thanks to an increase in mergers and acquisi-

25

tions. To get a clearer picture of how this affects individuals, though, meet Diane, who experienced it all firsthand.

Diane was a thirty-two-year-old editor of a national trade magazine when her publishing company was acquired by another firm. The new owner reassured everyone that no changes would be made. (Sound familiar?) Still, Diane was worried. "I just felt that things couldn't go on totally intact. Then, while researching an article for the magazine, I interviewed executive recruiters whose information confirmed my fears: They said that about 80 percent of management is fired or leaves when a company is taken over. Still, I figured if I continued to do an excellent job, I'd be safe."

Within a few months, though, Diane says that her publisher, who had always been very supportive, "suddenly started questioning everything I did. Before, I felt like we had a partnership; now I felt as if I were in enemy territory every time I came into the office.

"I started feeling really stressed and began getting sick a lot. Because of this, I started staying home and working out of my apartment. In hindsight, I think I was really avoiding the threatening office environment."

This situation went on for a few weeks until, one day, the publisher left this message on Diane's answering machine: "It's been decided that we will be hiring someone else as the magazine's editor. So don't bother coming in to the office again." And that was that. New management strikes again.

Incidentally, today Diana is running her own marketing and communications company and is "100 percent happier than I was at the magazine." Getting fired, she says, "gave me a chance to shift priorities and get my life more in balance. Before, my job was everything. Now I try to keep my work in perspective, to exercise, and to get together more often with family and friends."

(2) OFFICE POLITICS

We've all heard the phrase "office politics" bandied about so much that I think it merits closer examination.

There are three ways office politics can cause you to lose your job. The first is beyond your control—perhaps your boss is having an affair with your "future replacement," or the daughter of a major supplier has credentials similar to yours and she's just relocated to your town—whatever the reason, soon you're out in the cold.

The second kind of office politics is corporate politics. To understand it, think back to when you were a little girl playing a game with your big brother or sister. You usually lost, either because you didn't understand the rules at all or because you didn't understand them well enough so that they seemed to change whenever you pulled slightly ahead. The same holds true for corporate politics.

As Betty Lehan Harragan wrote in *Games Mother Never Taught You*, the world of business is like a "game board" where "explicit rules govern one's progress from place to place" and "penalties for unacceptable moves are swiftly enforced."

For a long time, women didn't recognize that business was a game. And even if they did, said Harragan, they were "apt to misjudge" which game was being played. "Consequently, many intelligent women can be found playing checkers while their opponents are playing chess. They have been able to identify a game board and certain playing pieces, but from there they extrapolate to simple games they know, failing to grasp the more complex moves allotted to certain pieces." Thus, she noted, women "get checkmated early in the game."

I love that last phrase—getting "checkmated." It's another wonderful euphemism for getting fired.

The third kind of office politics occurs when you *know* what the boss wants—how he wants you to act, who he wants you to act with—but you refuse to play along. And right or wrong, it costs you your job.

This actually happened to Lynne, my collaborator, so I'll let her tell the story.

"When I was teaching high school English, one of my worst students suddenly turned in a brilliantly incisive paper. I was certain she didn't write it herself, but just to be sure, I questioned her about the material. Clearly, it was not her work—she hadn't a clue about

27

the topic. But instead of failing her, which was my inclination, I gave her a chance to rewrite the paper on her own.

"The next day, I was called to the principal's office and asked if I couldn't be 'a little more lenient' with this student because her mother was a powerful member of the board and he, the principal, was up for tenure. Then he 'subtly' reminded me that my contract was also up for renewal.

"Well, I knew what he wanted me to do, but I refused to back down. Suddenly, my periodic evaluations, which had been excellent, became negative and picayune. Needless to say, I was not rehired for the following year."

"At the time, I was quite upset," Lynne recalls, "but in the long run, it gave me the push I needed to leave teaching and begin writing—a career that's brought me a whole lot more satisfaction."

(3) ECONOMICS

When business conditions improve, companies tend to expand staff, launch new advertising campaigns, and dole out such perks as paying for lunch when you work in or sending flowers on your birthday. But when the economic climate clouds, your birthday passes unacknowledged, you're on your own for lunch, and, much more significantly, management makes personnel cuts.

Barbara, a twenty-seven-year-old designer, fell victim to just such an economic downturn. Her company was having financial difficulties, but because it was headquartered in another state, she was unaware of the extent of the problem—until she returned from vacation and found a letter waiting in her mailbox.

"It turned out to be from the company president. He wrote that in my absence, a decision had been made to close the design room in my town. It was, he said, an economic decision and had nothing to do with my abilities as a designer. But the bottom line was that I was out of work.

"Great," says Barbara. "I had come back to my apartment to be fired by mail! Plus, it happened at a terrible time of the year, in early June, when it's more difficult to find a new position in my industry.

I was out of work until September, when I found a new spot. But let me tell you, it wasn't easy."

(4) PERSONALITY CONFLICTS

How many times have you met someone who rubbed you the wrong way—or vice versa? I know I have. But when that someone happens to be your boss, an influential colleague, or even the boss's secretary, you may be in for some rough going.

Sometimes it's because you and the other person simply don't like each other. You think she's a phony; she thinks you're over-bearing. But more often than not, it's an honest clash of work styles — that thwarts office harmony, as Victoria well understands. She was a seasoned media director for an advertising agency when she was wooed away by another firm.

At first, things went well. But soon a clear personality conflict between Victoria and her new boss became apparent. He was a cut-to-the-chase, bottom-line-results person, while she needed to antici-pate, discuss, and plan before she could produce. The problem came to a head when Victoria was given a particularly complex research project to oversee. True to her style, she kept arranging meetings with her boss to try to keep him abreast of the project's many pre-dicaments and to get his input. But the more she tried to involve him, the more angry and impatient he became—until one day he shouted, "All I want to know is that you'll get the work done!" Not surprisingly, Victoria lost her job.

WHO KNOWS WHY?

New management, corporate politics, economics, and personality conflicts are the most common reasons people get fired. There's one more reason, though, but I can't tell you what it is. Actually, nobody can. Because it occurs only when you've been fired for no apparent reason at all. Gloria is a perfect example.

She boasted a long list of professional credentials when she was hired as an administrator at a local hospital. Her diligence and expertise earned her a series of plaudits and promotions, culminating in her appointment to vice president, a position that carried a salary of nearly $80,000 plus a host of assorted benefits. Then, however, things changed.

"I was made a vice president in July and soon after decided to take a week's vacation. Three days after I returned, my boss said to me, 'I don't think you're viable here anymore.' I couldn't believe my ears, and asked him to repeat what he said. He did, and then it hit me: I'd been fired. He gave me no reasons, no explanations, nothing. I was stunned. It made no sense at all."

Gloria, who at age thirty-six had never failed at anything before, was devastated. "I felt so terrible that I couldn't function. Without a doubt, this was the worst experience I had ever had in my whole life. I thought, 'How will we pay the mortgage on the house? What am I going to do?' Emotionally, I just fell apart."

Gloria sought the advice of an attorney. "I live in an at-will state, so I really could not sue. But the attorney was able to help me negotiate a good severance package—nine months' salary, outplacement, and an excellent reference. Still, it did not begin to repay me for the emotional damage I suffered. And, although I've spoken with doctors and other personnel at the hospital, I never did find out why I was dismissed."

So You think You've Got Problems

Now that we've taken a closer look at *why* we get fired, let's see how. Most people are discharged during one quick, come-into-my-office conversation initiated by an immediate supervisor or a human resource manager. It's quick and painful—one exec I know calls it the "guillotine approach." But people can get fired in all sorts of ways, and I can't resist recounting at least a few of the more unusual stories I've heard.

THE DREAM SCENE

Among the strangest stories I've ever come across is Katie's. She was assistant to the president of a manufacturing company and doing an excellent job when the boss suddenly called her into his office. (Incidentally, it was first thing Monday morning. See, I told you early-bird meetings can be hazardous to your career health.)

Recalls Katie: "When I walked in, he looked up and said, 'I have something very personal and private to talk about. Last night I had a bad dream about you.' He wouldn't go into the details except to say it was very disturbing. Then he said, 'I was so upset that I went to a tarot card reader and learned something: The cards are not right between us. We cannot work together anymore. I'm letting you go.' " And with that, Katie was on the street.

And you think you've got troubles!

THE NOT-QUITE-SMOKING GUN

For three years, Delia worked as an attorney for a licensing company owned by a colorful, creative entrepreneur. She says, "He was the kind of person who meets someone at a party and does a deal right then and there. He was impulsive—and explosive, too. He'd do things like hire someone on the spur of the moment and forget to tell anyone else so that when the new person showed up, no one knew where he or she belonged.

"Then we heard through the office grapevine that he had started doing cocaine. I don't know if it was true, but I did notice that things became even weirder. He'd show up at the office barefoot, with his shirttails out; we'd find hookers waiting for him after work, and these big, tough-looking guys, probably bodyguards, started hanging around the office. And he started getting very paranoid, taking files off people's desks and grilling them about what they were doing.

"Things got pretty crazy and I wanted to quit, but my family and friends kept telling me not to unless I had another job. I was so stressed out that I couldn't even manage to look for anything else. So I really was in a bad spot.

"Then something happened that made things even worse: My immediate boss, the general counsel for the company, quit, which meant that I was now directly in the owner's line of fire. He started verbally abusing me, calling me into his office and criticizing me. Then one day he yelled, 'You are a stupid shit!'

"I couldn't believe it, but I said, relatively calmly, 'Well, if that's what you think then you probably don't want me working for you.' To which he replied, 'Right. You're fired!'

"Actually, I felt relieved—I thought the worst was over. But as I went into my office to pack up my stuff, one of those big, tough-looking guys I'd seen came in with a gun strapped across his chest. Apparently, he had been told to escort me to the elevator, wearing that gun!" It took Delia six months to get over the experience and feel strong enough even to begin to look for another job.

I'M FIRED? NO WAY!

On a more upbeat note, let me tell you my all-time favorite getting-fired story. Holly, a forty-year-old apparel merchandiser earning some $65,000 a year, loved her job. She says: "The job was great and I got along wonderfully with my boss. But I had always had problems with the company president. He resented me from the day I started.

"You see, when I was negotiating for this job, I had asked for a higher salary than the president wanted to offer. But because my two immediate supervisors were so high on me, they convinced him to give me the money I wanted. He did, but I felt he always held that against me. Whenever he'd get upset about something, I was always the one he railed against, whether or not I had anything to do with it.

"Anyway, one day he called me into his office and started carrying on about how things weren't working out, how there seemed to be many problems surrounding me, and how he had no choice but to make some changes and let me go.

"Well, when I heard that, something inside me just reared up. I looked him right in the eye and said, 'No, Bernie, you are not going to fire me.' I mean, I just wasn't *ready* to be fired!

"He just sat there as I proceeded to tell him all the reasons why he could not dismiss me. I kept talking and talking; every time he gave me a reason for wanting to fire me, I told him why he could not. This went on until we were not really talking but sparring. I guess I eventually wore him out, because finally he said, 'Okay. I'll think it over and let you know first thing in the morning.' "

Holly arrived "at the crack of dawn the next day. I was really nervous about this whole thing. But that SOB didn't call me in until noon, at which time he said, 'Okay. You can stay.' "

So she did, using the time to let people know she needed another job. Three months later, she was fired anyway. "But it was okay then—I was *ready* to be fired."

Holly's a really gutsy lady who's got the panache to carry off such a scenario. But I wouldn't advise it for the rest of us. Ninety-nine percent of the time, you'll lose the job anyway. But more about that later. For now, let's give Holly a well-deserved round of applause and move ahead to "firings of the rich and famous."

Fired and Famous

Remember how embarrassed and humiliated you felt when you got canned? Well, consider for a moment how much worse it would have been if a few dozen colleagues, acquaintances, and even enemies had been listening at the door. Now stretch your imagination further and think about how you'd feel if your firing made the front page of newspapers and magazines around the country!

Linda Ellerbee, the spunky, spirited, television journalist, doesn't have to imagine; she's been through it several times. Take her "extraordinarily humiliating" dismissal from the Associated Press newswire in Dallas.

While sitting at the AP desk one day, Linda had written a personal letter on the office word processor in which, as she puts it, "I maligned a couple of Texas newspapers, the Dallas city council, and a fellow I was dating, topping it off with a little something about a mutual friend." Accidentally, the letter went out over the AP wire in four states. Linda was fired, but, she says, "only because the AP's legal department told them it absolutely was against the law to shoot me, no matter how good an idea it was." To say the least, she felt awful.

"You know the old saying about how home is where they have to take you no matter what you do? Well, after that, I called my parents and took the next flight to Houston to see them. I remember that there was this terrible storm—lightning had hit the plane and people were screaming and throwing up. And I remember thinking, 'This doesn't scare me. What happened at AP scares me.' Now, rationally this is ridiculous because losing your job is not as important as losing your life. But that's how bad it felt. I remember I half wished the plane would go down—that's how strong the humiliation was."

Over the years, Linda was forced to weather other firings, called "cancellations" in TV lingo. But her self-described "cruelest blow" came while she was at NBC. "My book (*And So It Goes*) was just about to come out. Also, there was new management at NBC— General Electric had bought the network—and they were not fond of me. Unfortunately, my contract was among the first to come up for renewal and I think they intended to make an example of me so that when other contracts came up, people would either leave or take a big pay cut."

Technically, Linda was not fired from NBC; the network offered her a new contract, but with a 40 percent decrease in pay. Still, as she had when she'd been terminated, Linda felt "run out. I had been with NBC for eleven years, had survived four presidents—this new one was the fifth. And even though I had another job offer at twice the pay, and even with all my background and experience, I began to question myself. In a sense, this time was the hardest. I mean, with AP at least there was that letter. But here, I felt there was no cause and I felt I had done good work."

Looking back, Linda doesn't regret her firings; in fact, she feels they have taught her some valuable lessons.

"Someone once described me as having 'failed my way to the top,' and in a sense, it's true. I believe you grow more in failure than you do in success. And you learn that you find your strengths."

* * *

Sally Jessy Raphael, nationally syndicated TV talk show host, radio personality, and author, has been fired so many times—eighteen, to be exact—that she's developed a philosophy of dismissal: "Firing is a time to take assessment, to move in the direction you want to go. And as long as you have your hat in hand, I believe that you shouldn't try for less, but for more. More is as easy to get."

I love that phrase: "More is as easy to get." Let it be your mantra when you go on your next interview or enter into negotiations for your next job. And for Sally, it's proved absolutely true.

She approached each postfiring career situation believing that "the next employer has to pay for the last person's mistake." And it's worked. As Sally herself says, "I've always been fired into a better job."

Happy endings notwithstanding, every one of her job losses took its toll, especially since each was in broadcast media and was, thus, very public. "You feel like a national failure. You get that I-can't-go-out-in-public-because-I'm-a-failure feeling. A few times after I'd been let go, people came up to me and said, 'Didn't you use to be Sally Jessy Raphael?' " Talk about losing your identity!

For Sally, the discomfort of getting fired starts before she actually gets the boot. In fact, she notices a pattern of reactions that begin well ahead of the day she's told to clean out her desk.

"First, I begin to sense that things aren't going well, so there's tension that begins on the one hand. On the other hand, there's denial. That's where I say to myself that I know I'm good and that they really won't let me go. But even as I'm saying that, somewhere inside me there's a warning signal that says 'Something's wrong.' So there's a tremendous amount of anxiety before.

"Then, once I'm fired, I experience a burst of elation, a sense of relief because I've felt it coming. I get this tremendous adrenaline rush and I become a whirlwind of activity—cleaning out my desk, making a million phone calls, that kind of stuff.

"I also become particularly funny, because in my life I've always met adversity with humor. So after I'm fired, I joke more, I laugh more, become funnier. But really, I'm using the humor to cover up my tears. Finally, about five or six days afterward, I get that I've-been-punched-in-the-gut feeling."

Interestingly, Sally has always pushed herself to find another job fast. The reason? Money. "Up until just a few years ago, I'd never put any money away. So I had to start that income coming in as soon as possible."

(Actually, financial need is often a blessing in disguise to the involuntarily unemployed. I've noticed that women who have too soft a financial cushion get lazy about job hunting. It's amazing how having to make mortgage payments serves as a *serious* career prod.)

For Sally, two job losses stand out as being particularly difficult. One came just after she'd gotten her first radio show on WMCA in New York. "After the elation of having my own show in the number-one market died down, I realized that the woman who owned the station and I were not a match. Whenever we would go to business meetings, we were always going in different directions. Though it was clear that we were not meant to stay together, it took her five years to fire me. That was pretty awful. It was the longest time I had to wait for the other shoe to drop."

Sally's other difficult firing, outstanding because it was so "devastating," occurred when she was anchoring WPIX News in New York.

"I knew they were not happy with me, but what I did not know is that the station had told Pat Harper that anytime she wanted her job back she could have it. And, after eleven months, that's what happened. But it was what led up to my firing that was particularly devastating. That is, they handled me in a Christine Kraft–like manner. First they said 'You're too fat,' then 'You're too thin.' Then 'Your hair is too short,' then 'It's too long,' and on and on, personally criticizing me until I was completely worn down. I lost total confidence in myself."

As demoralizing and upsetting as these and her other very public firings were, Sally has always left with her dignity intact. She comments: "You know, when you're on radio and TV you have a lot of power for revenge. You could go on the air and say that these guys are firing me and they're bastards. But I had made a decision that I was going to conduct myself as a lady, so on my last day, I always thank the audience and the people who had brought me to them in the first place. And I do this because you meet the same people going around again. If I could pass along only one piece of advice to your readers, it would be this: No matter how bad your firing is, exit with style. You can go home and curse them out. But always exit gracefully." Thanks, Sally.

How It Feels on
the Other Side of the Desk

Sally's advice is well taken because it reminds us of something we often forget—that the person on the other side of that desk is a human being. I know if I asked you to name the five people in your life you most want to lock into a small closet with a 250-pound convicted felon named Bubba, the person who fired you would surely top the list. But did you ever stop to consider what your boss—I mean your ex-boss—was going through?

I'm not asking you to feel sorry for him or her, or even to forgive. But I do think that if you understand the point of view and emotional state of the person who's doing the firing it may help to diffuse a little of your anger and give you important insights and confidence. So set your feelings aside for a moment and listen to these comments from executives on the other side of the desk. I think you'll be surprised by what they have to say.

"The first time I had to fire someone I was a wreck," admits Marcia Gillespie, former executive editor of *Ms.* magazine. "I remember calling my former boss at Time Inc. and saying 'How do I *do* this?' I didn't sleep at all the night before, and, to tell you the truth, that's been true in most cases.

"You know, you're aware of how that person is going to feel even if you've warned them—the shock, the anger, the loss of self-esteem, fear. In many instances, you feel anxiety and guilt. I mean, who wants to be the bad guy?"

Joseph DeGennaro, director of human resources for Coopers & Lybrand, often coaches company managers who must fire members of their staff, and he confirms Marcia's point of view. He says: "The manager is anxious over having to fire someone and feels a sense of guilt, whether or not it's deserved. It's a very uncomfortable situation for them. And that's especially true because firing someone is a skill for which managers don't get much training."

For Bernadette Mansur, who worked for fifteen years as a marketing and public relations executive with Avon, the most difficult kind of firing is "letting someone you hired go. You feel you have more responsibility for that person, so you really feel guilty. That aside, though, you have to take the responsibility for your action and deal with the person honestly."

Just in case you haven't realized that guilt and anxiety are the overriding emotions of the person who's giving you the ax, listen to what Harriet Michel, president of the National Minority Supplier Development Council Inc., has to say about discharging employees.

"It's tough each and every time you fire someone. There's this person with a family and a life on the other side of your desk and you know, especially if you have been fired yourself, as I have, that what you're going to do is going to damage their self-esteem. I mean, you'd have to be a pretty mean-spirited person not to feel something."

Often employers, particularly the well-meaning, sensitive ones (yes, hard as you might find that to believe right now, there *are* well-meaning and sensitive bosses out there), feel a sense of sadness and failure when they have to fire you. As Carolyn Gottfried, founder of Gottfried and Loving public relations, says, "I feel less anxiety than sadness when I have to let someone go. When you hire someone, there are great expectations on both sides. When you fire someone, there's a sense of failure on both sides."

All this sensitivity and emotion may be hard to believe, especially if you're still smarting from firing's sting. But honestly, most employers *do* feel bad when they have to let you go. And guilty. And anxious. So as opportunistic as it sounds, keep their vulnerability in mind when I start telling you how to go ahead and ask your boss for whatever you think you deserve once you've been terminated. (We'll cover that in chapter 4.) After all, all's fair in love, war and getting fired.

How to React When You're Fired

In the course of my running WIN Workshops, I've come across lots of women who sheepishly confess to me, "When I got fired, I cried. I know it's terrible, and that you're never supposed to cry in an office, but I was so overwhelmed, it just happened."

Once and for all, let me answer the question inherent in their confession—Was it so terrible to cry?—with this: No. Of course, it's always preferable to remain as calm, rational, and professional as possible. But unless you got absolutely hysterical, the image that your ex-boss created of you over the long haul will survive the firing episode. However, displaying your anger by yelling or attacking (verbally or otherwise) your former boss might irreparably damage your image. What's more, such an outburst will only serve to reinforce what a good idea firing you really was.

It's also not in your best interest to ask for another chance. Holly's story notwithstanding, such second chances just don't work. Most of the time your request to be allowed to stay will be turned down, so you'll feel rejected twice. And even if you do get another shot, you and your boss will be bringing so much tension, anxiety, and resentment to the situation that it will be difficult if not impossible for you to work together effectively. Sooner or later you'll lose the job anyway. So don't ask to try again. Just chalk it up to experience and move on.

The other message voiced by executives, human resource personnel, other firees, and, of course, me, is this: The best reaction to being fired, and the one that will make the boss more amenable to any requests you might have, is not to react at all. Remaining cool and collected will strengthen your negotiating position, leave the impression that you're a consummate professional, and keep you from burning any unnecessary bridges. Remember what Sally Jessy Raphael said about exiting gracefully?

39

If, however, you've already lost your job and your cool, forget about it. Just tuck my little piece of advice into some corner of your brain so you'll have it available when and if you get another pink slip in the future.

Even as you're taking positive action toward your job search using the WINbreakers I discussed in the previous chapter, you may feel you need some guidance in coping with the emotional and psychological issues of being fired. Read on.

3.

The Mourning After

Check any and all that hit home:

☐ Ever since THE DAY, I've been waking up in a cold sweat at 2:00 A.M. worrying, "Will I ever work again?"

☐ I had them fooled on my last job, but now I've been found out.

☐ Will my age work against me in getting a new job?

☐ How will I ever explain this in an interview?

☐ Will I have to take a huge pay cut at my next job?

☐ I worry about where the rent/mortgage/kids' tuition money will come from.

☐ I secretly fear I'm going to become a bag lady.

☐ If I *do* land another job, do I have what it takes to hold on to it, or will this happen *again*?

☐ My colleagues are probably laughing behind my back.

☐ I feel like a failure.

If you've checked even one of the above, welcome to the club. I agonized over many of the same things after I was fired. And my talks with hundreds of just-dismissed women around the country showed me I had plenty of company.

That's why I've written this chapter: to let you know right away that you're not alone in your anxiety and fear. Getting fired is difficult for everyone.

But don't just take my word for it. Listen to what these WIN Workshop participants said after they got their walking papers.

Ellen, a forty-two-year-old executive who was fired from her $75,000+ a year position as company president, remembers: "I was so shocked about being fired that I accepted it as if my ex-boss had said, 'Isn't the weather lovely?' I was being such a good sport, yet inside I was scared to death—I was so hurt I really couldn't respond.

"When I was twenty-two, I was amazingly humorous and carefree about job hunting. But at this point, I almost forgot how to laugh. I felt very self-conscious and, most of all, I realized I didn't have a direction anymore."

Thirty-five-year-old Tracy, an assistant creative director earning $48,000 annually when she was fired, says: "The bad feelings I lived through after I was fired were the most demoralizing I ever experienced. I felt depressed, a sense of total worthlessness, and really low self-esteem. I hated it!"

The last comment comes from Jane, a forty-one-year-old trade journal editorial director who had been earning $55,000 annually. "I couldn't believe this was happening. Why hadn't I seen the handwriting on the wall? This job had been my family—getting rid of my husband had been easier! Now I felt alone and lost. I went home and cried. Soon after, I became angry. I didn't know where to turn and who to turn to."

The message rings out loud and clear: Getting fired is very painful. That's probably why we've invented so many euphemisms to refer to the "F" word. You've been "laid off," "terminated," "canned," "dumped," "axed," "given your walking papers," "pink-slipped," "excessed," "downsized," "sacked," or "de-jobbed." Call it what you will, though, everyone who's ever been employed has feared, with or without reason, that the dreaded scarlet "F" would be stamped mercilessly and indelibly on his or her résumé.

Growing legions of workers today are seeing their fears of being fired materialize. In 1988 alone, over 3.1 million workers in the United States lost their jobs; approximately one third were women.

What's more, the economy shows no signs of letting up on such "job losers" (that's the Bureau of Labor Statistics' term, not mine). It no longer matters what business sector you work in; white-collar workers have joined their blue-collar counterparts in the ranks of the involuntarily unemployed. And here's an unnerving statistic: Steve Harrison, president of Lee Hecht Harrison outplacement firm, predicts that 90 percent of all executives now in the work force will be given their walking papers *at least once* in their careers!

Still think you're alone?

On the Firing Line: Why Women Get Shot Down

Managerial women, as opposed to managerial men, are particularly vulnerable to being fired. I'm mostly referring here to the individual, "it's-Friday-afternoon-please-come-into-my-office" firing, not the massive corporate downsizing in which anyone can get caught in the crossfire. But even in corporate restructuring, when large numbers of employees are dismissed, women get hit the hardest.

There are several reasons for their vulnerability. First, women tend to build careers in such support fields as public relations, communications, marketing, and merchandising. Our regrettable relative lack of bottom-line responsibility in such areas as finance, sales, and production makes us extremely vulnerable when the cutbacks come.

Second, it is only within the last two decades or so that significant numbers of women have entered the work force. Riding the crest of the most recent feminist movement, many of us joined the ranks of middle and upper management, claiming titles such as vice president and director and earning significantly higher salaries than we ever had before. Accordingly, business schools' female enrollment soared. For example, at Columbia University Graduate School of Business, only 3.8 percent of the class of 1972 were women; by 1988, that number had leaped to 32.8 percent.

Yet despite our rapid success, or maybe because of it, many of us remain naive to the downside of corporate position and power. Still outside the good-old-boy network and relatively unschooled in playing corporate political games, many of us are finding ourselves with our backs against the wall, unable to wedge ourselves out of the way when the economic climate shifts and the ax starts swinging.

Moreover, it's no surprise to anyone that women are the object of sexual discrimination on the job. In the good-old-boy network, women are all too often considered expendable. "Their husbands can always support them" is the way the thinking, incredibly enough, still goes.

Not only are women highly vulnerable to being fired, they have an extremely tough time dealing with it. Through WIN Workshops, I've seen firsthand the way in which hundreds of top-drawer professional women react. Most of these women have stepped lively along seemingly charmed career paths; many earned incomes of between $35,000 and $100,000 a year. But today, now that they're in their thirties, forties, and even fifties, they are facing a brand-new experience—getting fired—and they're ill-equipped to deal with the emotional consequences.

In her landmark book *Games Mother Never Taught You*, Betty Lehan Harragan shed light on this issue. She wrote: "Men, too, suffer disappointments during a long business career, but their reactions are qualitatively different. As a rule, they are not dumbfounded by the experience. Their response is more likely to be summed up as, 'I knew that bastard would do this to me if he ever got the chance.' They foresee outcomes, understand why something happens, accept consequences. They are seldom crushingly surprised."

The way I like to explain it is that men tend to externalize when they get fired. They blame the system, the company, and other people *before* they blame themselves. Women, on the other hand, tend to internalize. We immediately think: "What did I do wrong? It must have been my fault. How could I have been so stupid?" (Or "pushy," "passive," "naive," "unthinking"—you supply the adjective.) We say to ourselves, "If I had only done things differently, I wouldn't have lost my job!" We may fuss and fume about our boss, but in our heart of hearts, we suspect that the real problem was ourselves.

I tell you what else women do differently. Women make their office a *home*, with the concurrent emotional attachment that implies. Haven't you ever heard a job-hunting friend say, "I'm looking for a new home"? Maybe that's what you're thinking right now.

Linda Eidelberg, a psychotherapist specializing in women and work issues, explains this further. "Women need to be liked and are more sensitive to rejection; they don't want to be alone. So they establish a connection by making their office a home."

One of the ways in which we do this is by "decorating" our offices. I know I did this to the extreme. Whenever I started a new job, I could have called the Santini Brothers to move me into my office. An antiques maniac, I brought in antique posters to hang, a collection of sixty snow shakers (those little glass or plastic domes with miniature scenes that you turn upside down to envelop in a snowstorm), an extraordinarily heavy antique oak coffee table, and old candy store jars that I kept filled with goodies for my staff.

You may not have gone this far, but chances are you brought lots of personal mementos and knickknacks to your old office—pictures of your kids or dog, a favorite coffee mug, a vase for flowers, souvenirs from your last vacation, some plants, a candy dish. Not to mention what you'd stashed in the drawers—extra pairs of shoes, boots, umbrellas, panty hose, nail polish, nail file, hair dryer, tampons, aspirin, antacids, makeup, deodorant, perfume, trail mix or another kind of snack. The fact is, if you had ever gotten locked in your office after closing, you would have been fairly comfortable. How many men do you know who could say the same thing?

It's not surprising then that when women get fired they're often devastated. For many of them, losing their job means more than losing a title, a position, money, or even power—it means losing a home.

Compounding this is that many women see their co-workers as *family*. Even those who make a concerted effort to keep their professional and social lives separate—by adhering to such self-imposed rules as not dating men from the office, for example—tend to build personal relationships with co-workers. They transform colleagues into friends or go so far as to play mother to their subordinates. Thus, when they get fired and have to leave the firm, it's all the more hurtful.

Explains Linda Eidelberg: "Women often have trouble with separation, with standing alone. So they overdo friendships at the office. Now there's nothing wrong with building relationships there, but you need to set up boundaries or at least be aware of the dangers of not having them.

"Too, when women get fired, instead of getting angry at the person who fired them, which would set them apart from that person, and, again, make them stand alone, they get angry at themselves."

Look, I know that making generalizations based on gender is dangerous, because there's an inherent risk of stereotyping. So let me say clearly that, of course, individual differences do exist; undoubtedly, some men find being fired *more traumatic* than some women do. Such differences notwithstanding, though, I'll stick to my guns and say that, based on my experience, women in general do have a different reaction to and often a more difficult time coping with being terminated than men do. So if you're a woman and you know you're not taking your firing "like a man," you're right. But so what? You're in good company, as the rest of this chapter, and indeed this book, will demonstrate.

The Emotional Stagecoach

I don't like Westerns—my affection for the Old West begins and ends with a great pair of jeans and tooled leather boots. But there is one image that I do like because it has particular relevance to being fired—the stagecoach.

It was called that because its journey consisted of several parts, or stages. Once you boarded, you were carried away on an uncomfortable, bumpy sojourn. You eventually got where you wanted to go, but not before you made several scheduled, predictable stops in places you usually would have preferred not to visit.

When you get fired, you're put aboard an emotional stagecoach. In time, it will bring you to your ultimate destination: that terrific new position or career. But first, you have to pass through some painful emotional stages that lie in every firing's wake.

Until this book, little had been written about the psychological consequences of being fired; however, much has been said about the emotional stages of loss. Kübler-Ross talked about them in the widely acclaimed book, *On Death and Dying*. Carole Hyatt and Linda Gottlieb showed how these stages apply to the feelings of loss that surround failure in *When Smart People Fail*. And since I believe that getting fired is usually viewed as both a failure and a loss, these emotional stages—shock, fear, anger, shame, and despair—are well worth examining now.

In their book, Hyatt and Gottlieb note that these stages "appear to be 'negative' ones in that they are painful, tumultuous and seemingly unhelpful. However, these 'negative' phases of failure actually perform a positive function. Like the steps in mourning, to which they are in many ways similar, the stages of failure force us to accept our loss and prepare us for the task of rebuilding."

True enough. But since getting fired is a particular kind of failure, let's take a look at how these stages apply to job loss.

SHOCK

You come into the office expecting business as usual. You've got a staff meeting planned that afternoon, you're involved in a million and one projects, and your appointment book has no white space showing for the next three weeks. Then, suddenly, you're summoned to your boss's office and the door is closed. You know what happens next.

After you hear the fateful words, you feel numb, dazed, disoriented. We've all experienced it, that is-this-really-happening-to-me feeling. For a few moments, you think you didn't hear your boss correctly, that you're really not fired and it's all a misunderstanding. Or, at the very least, it's April Fool's Day in June, July, February. . . . But soon you realize it's all very real.

That doesn't mean you're not still in shock. It takes time for you to absorb all the information and the impact it's going to have. And even though you think you're functioning normally, in reality you're not. But that's to be expected. Shock is your psyche's way of cushioning the blow.

FEAR

Initially, fear is often tied up with money—the "M" word. I call it that because so many women have so much trouble dealing with anything that has to do with money. We hate to ask for it; even more, we hate to argue about it. But we panic when it's denied us.

In rapid fire, financial fears race through our minds: "How am I going to pay the rent? How will we pay for Janie's braces? I can't believe I just splurged on a new designer suit I can't return. How will we make our car payments?"

In our survey, nearly 75 percent of just-fired women around the country said that loss of income was among the most difficult things to cope with after getting fired. Most expressed enormous concern even when there was a second family income from a husband or live-in companion.

Another major reason we become so gripped by fear when we lose our job is that so many things are out of our control. Such helplessness threatens our very sense of safety and well-being. As psychologist and stress expert Kenneth Frank, Ph.D., explains: "If you think about the process of adaptation and survival, you can understand this better. As infants, we have an extraordinary amount of complex information to process—sights, sounds, smells, touches, and so forth. Our feelings of safety and security in the world have to do with our learning to master our environment. When we cannot master it because circumstances are out of our control, it signals danger." We automatically respond by either fighting the danger or fleeing from it; in psychological lingo, it's called the "flight or fight response." That is, when we get fired, some of us may "fight." We immediately send out hundreds of résumés, make zillions of phone calls, and get ourselves mobilized to defend ourselves against this threat.

Sometimes, though, we react with flight; that is, we try to escape the danger. Psychologically, we say to ourselves, "It's Friday, and most people leave early, so I'll just wait till Monday to call." Or we say, "It's June, no one hires until September, so I might as well take the summer off." Or we decide we deserve a vacation and literally flee—catching the next flight out to wherever. Anything to avoid looking for a job.

Physiologically, flight can take the form of illness. Many times in my workshops, which meet over a six-week period, members miss sessions because they've got the flu, their backs are out, or they've got a migraine. Just as it did when we were little girls and our moms wouldn't let us skip school unless we had a fever, getting sick gives us a legitimate excuse to crawl into bed and go to sleep. Maybe, we subconsciously think this nightmare of getting fired will disappear when we wake up.

ANGER

Anger can be directed at many different targets. Often, the target is the boss and/or the company, or someone within the firm whom you believe sabotaged your job. You think about all the hours you put in, all the time and energy you invested—how dare they fire you!

Most recent firees experience anger. In rare and extreme instances, the feeling becomes so intense that the ex-employee goes back to the office and trashes the place. The vast majority of us, however, take out our anger in healthier ways. We go home and cry our hearts out into our pillows. We bitch to our best friend. Or we fantasize that the company will crumble without us. What made me feel better was putting hexes on those people I held responsible for my predicament. I'd envision them off on a business trip; their plane would be hijacked and they would be tortured unmercifully. (I've never told this to anybody before, so let it be our little secret, okay?)

49

Often, though, we don't direct our anger outwardly, at the company or the boss, but inwardly, at ourselves. We blame ourselves for not seeing the warning signs and being so vulnerable to this blow. Frequently, we blame ourselves for screwing up and causing our own firing. It doesn't matter whether or not we actually were at fault; we beat up on ourselves anyway. We feel stupid and incompetent, and our self-esteem plummets.

In fact, when we asked our survey respondents, "What was the toughest thing to handle about getting fired?" nearly one third put lack of self-esteem at the top of their list. What's more, just under 70 percent ranked it first, second, or third. Apparently, this is the second stickiest problem to handle, next to loss of income.

It may perk you up a bit to hear what Atlanta management psychologist Neil P. Lewis, Ph.D., says about getting fired. Often, he reports, "a firing represents a bad hire, a bad transfer. In many cases, it is a failure of management."

I'm not saying that you never have to share responsibility for getting fired. Maybe you didn't play the game by the company rules, or perhaps you were promoted to a position for which you were not qualified. But only in rare instances is it *totally* your fault. Think about that the next time you start trashing yourself.

SHAME

Once your self-esteem takes a nosedive, you're ripe for stage four, shame. Marilyn Puder-York, Ph.D., a psychologist whose Wall Street practice has seen an upsurge in the formerly employed, explains it this way: "When you see your firing as a personal loss, one that is your fault, you will feel a sense of shame and embarrassment. Also, when you see being fired as tantamount to failure"—believing that you've let yourself, your parents, your spouse, your friends down— "you will feel a major sense of shame."

Barrie S. Greiff, M.D., consulting psychiatrist to Harvard University Health Services, tells us more: "We live in a culture where the job defines the individual. You go to a cocktail party and everyone asks, 'What do you do?' Because in our society, you are what you do. And that's what gets stripped from you when you get fired. You become vocationally naked and it feels bad."

But as Hyatt and Gottlieb note in their book: "Shame is an unproductive feeling, but one that can only exist if you grant others authority to judge you. If you take back the judgment for yourself, if you like and forgive yourself, you cannot feel shame. No one can make you a victim but you yourself."

DESPAIR

Actually, I feel that despair is too strong a word when you're talking about getting fired. Not that some amount of helplessness and hopelessness doesn't hit us hard, because it does. But the great majority of women who've just gotten the ax experience something more akin to depression. Our spirits sag, and some days we drag around the house in our sweatsuits—that is, if we bothered to get out of bed at all. The highlight of our day is watching other folks complain about *their* sorry lives on *Oprah* or *Donahue*.

But let me pass along a bit of advice I offer at the first session of every WIN Workshop: Don't get down on yourself for getting down on yourself.

When you lose your job, it's perfectly normal to have bouts of depression mixed with anxiety, anger, or fear. We all go through it; after all, you've just experienced a major loss. As long as it doesn't go on too long, to the point where it prevents you from getting on with your life, give yourself permission to accept the feeling.

The stages we've just discussed provide a wonderful framework to help you understand what you're probably feeling these days. But they're not carved in stone. For instance, some people never feel shock; instead they feel relief either because in their heart of hearts they disliked their job and someone has now let them off the hook, or because they sensed the firing was coming (whether consciously or unconsciously) and were happy to see an end to the tension.

As Dr. Puder-York notes: "The stages of loss are a nice standard, but in my clinical experience, there are wide variations that depend upon several factors like how the job loss was communicated. If you're fired humanistically, where your self-esteem is preserved, you may never feel shame or self-blame. If you're given appropriate information and time to be proactive in planning your retrenchment, you may never feel anxious about being out of control."

Further, says Dr. Puder-York: "If you have adequate supports, family and friends, if you're not that invested interpersonally in the job, and if you're a person who adapts well to change, you may do better than someone else who does not share these characteristics."

The point is, everyone is unique. Even if the person who holds the same title as you and has the office next to yours is fired on the same day, it doesn't mean that you'll both go through this process in the same way, at the same pace, or with equal amounts of angst.

Post-Pink-Slip Predictor Test

To help you gain some important insights into the nuances involved in surviving the emotional trauma, I've invented a little test that will help you predict how you'll fare emotionally after you've gotten your pink slip. Accordingly, I call it the Post-Pink-Slip Predictor Test. Just grab a pencil and paper and give it a try.

Each category below represents extremes of the continuum, with 10 being the most positive (a strong "yes") and 1 being the least positive (a strong "no"). For example, look at the first question. If you're always optimistic and enthusiastic, you would give yourself a 10 (the highest rating). If you are always pessimistic, you would rate a 1 (the lowest rating). But suppose, like most of us, you're somewhere in between. You know yourself best; if you're basically an "up" person, but you do have your down days, you're probably somewhere between 7 and 9. If your tendency is to be negative most of the time, you could be a 2 or 3. Here's another example: If you're under 35, that's a plus in the work place; if you're over 50, that's a negative. You get the idea.

Don't spend much time on this; five minutes should do it. We're going for a gut reaction here, and your first response is usually the most honest and accurate.

Circle the number that best applies:

+					−				

1. I am generally optimistic. / I am generally pessimistic.

   10   9   8   <u>7</u>   6   5   4   3   2   1

2. I am financially secure (hefty severance, money in bank, family support). / I'm not sure I have the money to pay the rent.

   10   <u>9</u>   8   7   6   5   4   3   2   1

3. I have emotionally supportive spouse, family, friends. / I feel all alone.

   10   9   8   7   <u>6</u>   5   4   3   2   1

4. My firing was "friendly" (good severance, outplacement, caring personnel department). / My firing was sudden, cruel, and abusive.

   10   9   8   7   6   5   <u>4</u>   3   2   1

5. I'm under 35. / I'm over 50.

   10   9   8   7   <u>6</u>   5   4   3   2   1

6. I've changed positions or companies approximately every three to five years; in fact, I welcome change. / I was with my last firm over ten years; change makes me anxious.

   10   9   <u>8</u>   7   6   5   4   3   2   1

7. I maintained a balance between my work, social life, and outside interests. / I'm a workaholic.

   10   9   8   7   6   5   4   3   <u>2</u>   1

8. I've been fired more than once. / I've never been fired.

   10   9   8   <u>7</u>   6   5   4   3   2   1

+					−				

9. My industry is healthy and new opportunities abound.

My industry is depressed and jobs are scarce.

10	9	8	7	6	5	4	3	2	1

10. Other than being unemployed, life is good.

I'm going through a divorce, taking care of an ill/dying parent, coping with a substance abuser in the family, or dealing with one of life's other stressors.

10	9	8	7	6	5	4	3	2	1

Before I tell you what your score means, I want to make something clear. This test is not intended to make you think, "Oh, getting a new job will be a snap," nor is it meant to make you wring your hands in despair; neither of those reactions will be helpful. Instead, use this test to gain insight into the factors that will affect your ability to cope with your jobless state.

And remember that, whatever your score, this book will help. It will give you the support, skills, confidence, and courage you need to go out there and get the job you most want. But first you've got to understand yourself as thoroughly as possible—what you want, what you feel, and what you need. And understanding your test results will help you begin.

Now add up your answers and calculate your score. If it totals 100, congratulations! Go give this book to a friend who *really* needs it.

If your score is 75 to 99, you're in pretty good shape. You might not be feeling great about yourself right now, but you have enough pluses in your life to help get you through this transitional period.

A score of 50 to 74 indicates that this period may be pretty tough for you, especially if you scored low on Question 2, 3, 5, 9, or 10. You should find this book especially helpful, so read every page carefully. You may also benefit from joining a women's support group or from starting one of your own. I'll tell you how to do that later in this chapter.

If your score is under 50, you may want to consider not only relying on friends and family to get you through, but seeking the guidance of an experienced professional as well. Go to someone you're comfortable with or whom you believe can offer some sound advice, such as a religious leader or career counselor. It may be appropriate to consult a mental health professional such as a psychologist or psychiatrist. This doesn't have to mean long-term therapy; sometimes a few sessions can make a difference.

Managing Your Stress

Now let me tell you why all this insight into your postfiring emotions is so important. First and foremost, it will make you feel less alone and reassure you that what you're feeling is perfectly normal. Second, and equally important, it will help you manage the stress of being fired and lessen the risks to your health.

No kidding. Getting fired could be harmful to your health. And not just your emotional health.

Harvey Brenner, Ph.D., and professor in the Behavioral Sciences Department at Johns Hopkins University, has conducted a series of studies on job loss and its most extreme effects. He's found a statistically significant relationship between job loss and state mental health admissions, mortality from cardiovascular and renal disease, cirrhosis of the liver (often brought about by excessive drink—drowning your job-loss sorrows), and even suicide.

This kind of stress can also cause less severe but nonetheless upsetting difficulties, including trouble sleeping, a greater susceptibility to colds, headaches, high blood pressure, and stomach problems.

Stress can also throw you into the "lost-key mode." When you're under stress and preoccupied with the job of looking for a job, you're more likely to lose your keys (hence the term "lost-key mode"), to become accident-prone or fumble-fingered. (Pam had to buy a set of plastic dishes in order to protect her good china from total destruction!) You're also more likely to be pickpocketed, because, I've been told, a professional pickpocket can spot that preoccupied look a mile away.

So much for the bad news. The good news is that if you understand a little about emotional trauma and have a bit more insight into the way you personally will be affected by it, you can do a great deal to avoid the more severe consequences.

Here are a few things I prescribe to women suffering from the pink-slip blues:

• Keep physically active. Exercise will recharge your body and give you the kind of psychological kick-start you need during this stressful period. It can be as simple and inexpensive as walking. If you miss the camaraderie of the office, joining a gym and participating in classes might be especially helpful.

• Avoid alcohol, caffeine, and sugary or fatty foods. Eating healthfully will keep your energy level high; gaining weight might make you feel more depressed or out of control. You have a lot to do now, and you'll do it best if you're operating at peak efficiency.

• Create a routine and stick to it. I know how seductive it can be to pull the covers over your head and sleep late. After all, you don't have a job anymore, so why not?

I'll tell you why not. Lack of structure and routine is one of the most stressful aspects of being fired. It's totally enervating and will serve to deepen any depression you might be feeling. So force yourself to get up at a certain time every morning and set a few tasks for yourself. Some days that might mean sending out résumés and telephoning contacts; other days, it may just mean organizing your closets. But doing something productive daily will give your life some structure and make you feel more in control again.

• Read. At the end of this book, you'll find a bibliography. These are all terrific books and articles and have a wealth of information to offer. Look over the list and select those titles that you feel will help you most.

• Get your feelings out. Ask one or two close friend or family members to take some time to listen to your fears, complaints, and plans. Don't expect them to solve your problems, but just to serve as a sounding board for your deepest feelings. They're also a great source of hugs and comfort, and you need both right now.

• Join a support group, or start your own. You need to find a group of women who are going through the same thing you are at the same time. (I recommend women because their experiences and feelings will be more pertinent to yours.) If such a group already exists, that's great; sign up now. But if you can't find an established group, organize your own. That's how WIN Workshops started.

Start asking friends, neighbors, relatives if they know any other women who've recently lost their jobs. Local women's organizations may be able to give you good leads. Try to find women at or at least near the same professional level as you because the sessions will be more productive that way. Ideally, the group should have between five and ten people; over ten gets too unwieldy and doesn't permit everybody to talk at every gathering, and under five doesn't offer enough variety of personalities and ideas.

Meet at least once a week. Sessions can be as informal as you wish. Gathering at members' homes is fine; so is meeting at a inexpensive local restaurant or community center. Make sure the group has a leader. If you feel uncomfortable in that role, do make sure someone chairs the group and makes certain everyone knows when and where the meetings are being held, ensures that everyone's concerns are heard each week, and keeps the meetings productive through exchange of information and job leads.

For that first session, have everybody bring enough résumés to exchange with every other member of the group. Also, every time you meet, members should bring their personal and professional phone books—you never know who you know who can help another member.

On the first night, take some time to really get to know one another. Go around the room and have each person tell her firing story. You'll probably notice a lot of common themes. After everyone has had an opportunity to speak, open the floor for a general discussion centering on those common concerns.

Future weeks can focus on critiquing each other's résumés, setting up role-playing interviews, and networking—here's where those phone books come in handy. Another helpful project is to have different members read specific books from the recommended reading list, then summarize and review them for the group. This will save you some reading time and open up more topics for discussion.

Finally, if your group becomes an ongoing one, you might contact such local professionals as a career counselor, a psychologist, an executive recruiter, or even a lawyer and ask them to speak. Some may provide their services for free, so don't be afraid to ask. But if they do want a fee, splitting it with the group shouldn't pinch your pocketbook that badly.

• Give yourself some quiet time to think and reassess. I know I told you to stay busy, and you should. But try not to get frantic and schedule some activity for every minute of the day. As I've said, you need some time to take stock of what you really want out of your career. Considering what you're going through, you're entitled.

Now that you've recovered your emotional bearings, you're ready to begin your new job search in earnest. But first you need to set yourself up as best you can by negotiating your way out of your old job. Sound impossible? The next chapter explains how.

4.

Negotiating Your Way Out: Learning to Use the "M" Word

Of all the sessions that make up a WIN Workshop, the evening I devote to negotiating is by far my favorite. That's because it's the one in which everyone learns the most, the night we discuss money—the "M" word.

The reason I call it the "M" word is that "money" is a curse word to most women, something they feel uncomfortable discussing, let alone negotiating for. So I devote a whole evening—and two chapters in this book—to helping women understand what to ask for, how to ask for it, and most important, how to feel confident while doing both.

You'll need to use good negotiating skills twice after you've been fired: once when you're on the way out (yes, you can and you should negotiate your way out of the job) and again when you're on your way into a new company. I'll discuss the latter in chapter 9, but for now, let's concentrate on getting you out of your old job in the best possible shape.

Going Out a WINner

Most women are surprised when I use the words "negotiate" and "severance" in the same sentence. They always ask, "How much negotiating leverage can I possibly have after I've been fired?" To which I reply, "Enough."

Think of it from the other side of the desk. Most companies want to maintain a good image in the marketplace, and they don't want their ex-employees walking around bad-mouthing them. If a company does get a reputation for chewing up and spitting out workers, or becomes known as a revolving-door firm, it won't be able to attract the best people. Since new, high-caliber employees are a company's lifeblood, that's a serious problem. And one most firms try to avoid.

Also, a company has its remaining employees to consider. When even one person, not to mention an entire department, is let go, the people still working get anxious—and understandably so. But good firms realize that if the terminations are handled sensitively, with the concern of the ex-employee(s) in mind, then the spirit—and productivity—of those left behind won't be drastically damaged.

Another reason you have some negotiating leverage is that many companies fear a possible lawsuit. And although, as I pointed out in chapter 1, the odds are in their favor, any litigation (no matter the outcome) is time-consuming, costly, and often brings bad press. To stave off lawsuits brought about by disgruntled employees, companies may well be receptive to rethinking your severance package.

The last reason revolves around what severance is truly based upon—guilt. Believe it or not, there is such a thing as a corporate conscience, and it goes to work when someone is dismissed. (Unless, of course, the reason for the dismissal was gross misconduct, such as stealing, violent behavior, extortion, etc.)

The intensity of the firm's guilt is often based on a variety of factors:

- Length of employment: Dismissal of loyal, long-term employees or very short-term ones (clearly wrong hires, or possibly a hire away from another firm), will trigger corporate guilt.

- Level of employment: The higher up you are, the more guilt your ex-employer will feel because he or she knows you may have a more difficult time resituating yourself.
- Age: Employees over age fifty could also have a harder time repositioning themselves, so the company could be more receptive to taking care of them, too.
- Degree of specialization: Highly specialized employees with limited opportunities for reemployment may also be given special consideration.

Even if none of the above applies directly to you, your employer will possibly feel some guilt upon firing you. In all of the interviews we did with executives who have fired people, not one denied feeling guilty. So keep that in mind and use it to your advantage.

Two other factors influence whether you are able to walk out of your job a winner. First and most important is your company's mentality. A large, highly structured, publicly owned company is going to be less receptive to negotiation than a small, flexibly structured, privately owned business. Many corporations, particularly large ones, have their severance policies articulated in print. Making exceptions could set a precedent, which is something that such companies hate to do.

Conversely, a small firm with no such clearly stated rules leaves its door more open to exit negotiations. On the other hand, because a small company may have no written severance policy, legally it owes you NOTHING. Those unused sick days or vacation weeks are not owed to you unless you had it in writing.

The second factor influencing the negotiations is your own mentality. Tessa Albert Warschaw, Ph.D., and author of *Rich is Better*, calls it the Poverty Mentality. Many women's "unconscious decision to live an unfulfilled life" makes them believe that there's a limit to what they deserve to get. Not that you always get whatever you want; for instance, expecting one year's severance after six months of employment is unrealistic. But if your requests are sound, then you have a good chance of having at least some of them answered.

My negotiating motto is simple: You don't get what you don't ask for. So ask.

After the Ax: What to Ask For

At first, the best idea is to ask for nothing. Wait to hear exactly what your company is offering in the way of a severance package. Then, if you don't feel the offer is adequate, say something like "You've taken me by surprise; I really didn't expect this. I've heard what you're offering me, but I need some time to digest it. Can we set up an appointment in a day or two to discuss it further?"

It's true that in a downsizing or corporate restructuring you probably knew about the layoffs well in advance. But since you didn't know precisely what you would be offered, you have a right to request a day or so to think about the terms.

One unbreakable rule: Don't Sign Anything!

When you are fired, your company may ask you to sign some sort of agreement before you get your last check. It could be anything from a statement that you will not sue the company, to a promise that you won't work for the competition and/or won't hire away key employees for your next company, to an acknowledgment that the company has given you all monies it owes you. I urge you to wait until you've had time to get professional advice from a lawyer, accountant, or other qualified individual before signing anything.

Negotiating for Severance

If you're like most professional women, your company has already offered you some severance. But if you feel the amount is unreasonable, ask for more.

What's unreasonable? Well, suppose you were director of sales with the same company for nine years. When the president died, the vice president took over the reins and fired you with only two weeks' severance. *That's* unreasonable.

Now, suppose that after a four-year tenure at a small computer company, you received four months' severance plus an additional two weeks to make up for the vacation you never got to take. *That's a good deal.*

Our survey of professional women revealed more specific guidelines. In fact, we found a few patterns emerging:

- Almost all women who were fired after working one year or less received two weeks' severance.
- Companies with clearly delineated policies provided one week, two weeks, or at best, one month of severance for every year of completed service.
- Many larger companies provided a maximum of six months' severance, no matter how long the term of employment.

You have to remember, as I've said before, that the amount of your severance also depends on the level of your position and your perceived contribution to the firm. If you feel, however, that you've been treated unfairly, *even if your company has an "official" severance policy*, it's not unprecedented to negotiate for, and get, more. One vice president of human resources at a major manufacturing company told me that even though his company policy called for one week of severance per year, one particularly respected vice president whose position was phased out received two months' severance after only three years' employment.

Here's another instance: Amy had worked in promotion at a major newspaper for five years when she was hired away by a start-up publication that offered her a substantially higher salary and an impressive title. The job lasted all of two weeks. When the publisher fired her, he admitted the hire had been his mistake and said, "Even though you've only been here two weeks, we're still going to give you two weeks' severance."

When Amy told me about this, I urged her not to accept this "generous" offer. Had he not lured her away from another position with inflated talk of her wonderful future with his firm, she would never have been in this fix. Since her former company would have given her at least five months' severance, one for each of her years there, I encouraged her to call the publisher and set up an appointment. When they met, she told him that she felt the whole matter, both her hiring and her firing, was handled unprofessionally and that the severance was unacceptable. She explained her former company's policy and asked him to match it. Two days later, he agreed on a compromise of three months' severance. She'd done it: negotiated a WIN/win.

Negotiating for severance is not like antiquing, where each party names a figure and you meet somewhere in the middle. Just because you ask for more doesn't always mean you'll be as lucky as Amy and get it. Be prepared for that. But I'll say it once again: You don't get what you don't ask for.

There are ways to better your chances of negotiating a higher severance. "Say something that will make it appear that it will be hard for you to get another job," advises Madeleine T. Swain, president of Swain and Swain, one of the most respected outplacement firms in the United States. "For instance, if your company has relocated overseas, then let you go, and you want to return to the States, you could stress that your stateside contacts have dried up over the years you've been abroad and thus it could take you a long while to get another position. If your industry is depressed, you might emphasize that to explain why you need a stronger financial safety net."

Another way to increase your chances of getting more severance is to be as calm, rational, and objective as possible, clearly pointing out why you feel the company's offer is unacceptable. Offer strong reasons, like your long tenure with the firm, your contributions to the company (bringing in new accounts, saving the firm money), and, if appropriate, the particular circumstances surrounding your firing. Don't base your argument on personal need—for example, you just got a rent hike, your son is starting college, you're in the middle of renovating your home. Keep things professional, but make certain the firm understands how dissatisfied you are; it wouldn't hurt to make your soon-to-be ex-employer a little nervous.

Negotiating for Outplacement

Talk about guilt! Outplacement is an industry almost entirely based on it. The field began gathering speed during the recession of the seventies, when such labor-intensive industries as banking and insurance started to lay off many workers and wanted to both alleviate their guilt and forestall any possible lawsuits. The purpose of outplacement: to assist former employees in repositioning themselves.

Basically, there are two types of outplacement: group and one-on-one. Companies might arrange for group services for various levels of employees when there's been a massive downsizing. Group outplacement can range from a one-day, bare-bones seminar on how to write a résumé, begin a job search, and/or develop a target contact list, to a multi-day program with follow-up counseling. The kind of group outplacement offered is generally not open to negotiation.

On the other hand, one-on-one outplacement is. Usually, however, companies offer only senior executives the full menu of available services. Jane Antil, senior vice president of Goodrich & Sherwood, one of the largest outplacement firms in the nation, reports that a good outplacement company supplies such services as an office to use on a daily basis, secretarial assistance, unlimited access to a phone, and help in organizing, writing, printing, and even mailing a résumé to search firms nationwide. Antil says outplacement firms also supply career counseling and help in career assessment. When appropriate, some firms give spouse or family counseling. Full-service outplacement is very expensive, however, costing the company approximately 12 to 15 percent of the employee's base salary plus bonuses, which is why it's usually offered only to management-level employees on up.

However, Madeleine Swain notes that some sort of outplacement assistance can also be made available to other levels of employees. You might be able to negotiate for a one-shot individual counseling session or a longer-term program; it depends on the company's resources and the particular circumstances surrounding your dismissal. Madeleine has even come across one woman who had been the executive secretary to a high-level officer and was able to get outplacement when she was let go. But Madeleine warns: "I've also come across lots of companies who do not mention outplacement when they let someone go. But many of them will offer some form of it *if* an employee asks for it." So ask for it!

That's what Erica did. For ten years, she was the vice president of a privately owned company. When the firm went through a reorganization and decided it needed someone with a different set of skills, it let her go, offering six months of severance. After taking my workshops, Erica learned about outplacement, a word that had not been in her vocabulary until then. Although she had been fired two weeks earlier, she went back to her former boss and explained just how hard it would be to find another job because of her age (fifty-two) and area of specialization.

His reaction? "He agreed immediately," says Erica. "I think he was nervous about the possibility of an age discrimination suit, though I certainly did not threaten him with that. I also think he felt tremendously guilty. Anyway, by the end of our negotiations, I not only got one-on-one outplacement but three months' additional severance as well."

An interesting twist: Leigh was offered outplacement when she was fired from her job as senior vice president of production for a regional candy company. The day after she got fired, she called me to register for a workshop. During our conversation, she told me that although she had been offered one-on-one outplacement she had already arranged for three interviews and felt quite confident and optimistic about her job search. So I suggested that since in the company's view it had already spent the money on her outplacement—which at her salary level came to a substantial amount—she should ask for that amount in lieu of outplacement. Sound improbable? Well, guess what? She asked for it and got it—an additional $25,000 added on to her severance.

Just a footnote: Certain kinds of industries, especially those that are people-intensive and concerned about their public image, such as banks and insurance companies, are more receptive to outplacement than businesses such as fashion, advertising, and certain forms of manufacturing. The latter kinds of firms don't tend to offer outplacement very freely at all, so keep that in mind if outplacement is among your list of "negotiating out" requests.

A Few More Negotiable Items

In addition to severance and outplacement, fired employees can negotiate for other concessions. Before you enter into outgoing talks, here are a few other things you could request:

A LETTER OF REFERENCE

Showing a potential employer a strong letter of reference from the person who let you go may serve to deflect a telephone reference check. It shows that you left on good terms and that your work was well respected.

But don't assume that such a letter will be given to you automatically. Almost all the human resource executives I've spoken with have said that, although they rarely refuse a request for one, they don't usually offer these letters.

Sometimes, you will be asked to write your own. If you are, don't be modest. Detail your major contribution to the firm and all your positive attributes, such as strong management skills, initiative, professional attitude—you get the idea.

This might also be a good time to script your reason(s) for leaving the company. Bill Morin, chairman and CEO of Drake Beam Morin, an international outplacement firm, recommends that you actually write down why you are no longer with the firm, show that statement to whomever you would like to use as a reference, and have him or her approve it. That way, if a potential employer calls for a reference check, you won't have to worry about what will be said.

OFFICE SPACE

You must have a base of operations from which to conduct your job search. As I've said, it's best if you can find an office of your own to work from, whether at a friend's company or in your home. But as a last resort, an office in your old company can be a lifesaver, even if it's only accessible for a few weeks. So if you need it, ask for it.

Do remember, though, that this is a last-ditch choice. I don't feel it's healthy to return to the same environment from which you've been fired. It will bring back bad memories and create some awkward situations with former colleagues. Even more dangerous, you can get caught up in believing that you're still working at your old company, a fantasy that can stop you from looking for a new job.

SECRETARIAL ASSISTANCE

I don't know about you, but when I lost my last job I couldn't type. Also, not everybody owns a typewriter or word processor. You will be astounded (or maybe not, having just read the previous chapters) by how much writing and correspondence you'll have to do—résumés, cover letters, follow-up notes—and all should be type-written or printed up on a high-quality computer printer. You might ask your former employer, therefore, if you can come in to the office for an hour once or twice a week for a specified period of time to have someone do your typing for you. Or better yet, see if your former company will pay for an outside professional typing service.

COMPANY CAR

If you've had a company car all along, you might want to ask to retain its use for a specified period of time while you're searching for a new job. There are lots of reasons you might give. If you live in the suburbs and the car you've been given is your only means of transportation, being car-less is the last thing you can afford right now. Unemployment is debilitating enough; being immobilized will just make things worse. As for buying a new car—ever try getting an auto loan when you're unemployed? Negotiating to keep your company car for a minimal amount of time, at least until you can make other transportation arrangements or find a new position, will be an invaluable aid.

UNUSED VACATION SALARY ADDED TO SEVERANCE

Unless it's otherwise spelled out in a company handbook, legally you're not entitled to unused vacation days. But if you haven't taken advantage of your allotted vacation time, then it doesn't hurt to ask to have your accrued vacation days added on as severance.

MEDICAL COVERAGE DURING SEVERANCE PERIOD

By now you're familiar with COBRA (see chapter 1) and know that you're entitled to remain covered by the company's group insurance plan (provided that you don't land a job with its own coverage) for eighteen months. During that time, under COBRA, you continue paying your own share and pick up the company's contribution as well. But you can negotiate for your company to reimburse you for its share during this period.

And here's another negotiating point. Let's say that you've been offered three months' severance. You can ask your company to set COBRA in action *after* your term of severance, as opposed to putting it into effect from your date of firing. This way you will have accomplished two things: first, you will have extended your group medical coverage to twenty-one months, and second, the company will be paying its share for an extra three months—which means more money in your pocket.

RELOCATION BACK HOME

Quite honestly, this is something that should have been discussed before you took your position, and I'll address it in greater detail in chapter 9. But if your ex-company relocated you away from your home base, and then let you go after a relatively short period of time—say, under two years—you should try asking for financial help moving back home. A reasonable request could include moving costs and assistance in selling your house or apartment.

CONTRACT PERKS

If you had a contract and/or a severance agreement, make sure you get all the perks you have coming to you. For instance, if you were promised an annual guaranteed bonus of 10 percent of your salary and you had a four-month severance agreement, then, in addition to getting your base salary for that four-month period, you should also get one third of that bonus as part of your severance. If your company was paying your graduate school tuition, then it should continue paying it over your severance period.

PENSION COMPENSATION

Madeleine Swain also advises fired employees to request compensation if they've lost a pension. The amount of dollars you can translate this into depends on your particular situation, so check with a lawyer or accountant if you believe this pertains to you.

I can't emphasize enough how important effective outbound negotiations are. Not only will they make you feel more in control, but very practically they could translate into thousands of dollars in your pocket—dollars you'll need as you begin the process of repositioning yourself.

So as difficult as renegotiating your severance may be, make a list of what you want—and go for it!

5.

At the Crossroads:
Careers Aren't Like Love

$\mathbf{Y}$ou know how when you meet a really great guy—we're talking Mel Gibson great here (well, a little taller; I'm five-nine)—your emotions seem to sweep you away? Without thinking about it, without any plan, forethought, or contemplation, you fall totally and completely in love.

The operative word here is "fall." Falling is terrific when you're talking about love, but not careers. Because careers aren't like love and you shouldn't just fall into them.

Unfortunately, though, many of us do. Several of my workshop participants, for instance, began their careers in retailing only because they took a summer job as a salesgirl. Over the years, one promotion led to another and they never left—never, that is, until they got fired.

Others hated to job hunt. Consequently, they stumbled into their careers by accepting the first position offered them.

And how about those teachers who entered the field only because their mothers told them, "It's a good career for a woman. When you get married and have children you can be home when they're home and have your summers off. And you'll always be able to get a job." Many of them never liked teaching and now, twenty or so years later, feel bored, underpaid, burnt-out, and, often, trapped.

Whatever the scenario, the common theme is that many of us simply fell into our careers at some point in our past. Even women who deliberately chose a career early in their professional lives may now find that things have changed—they've changed—and they're no longer satisfied. Still, they feel they must stick to the field in which they've accumulated all their experience.

But let me say this about ill-chosen or ill-fitting careers: They set you up to fail. That's why it's so important to take some time to stop and think about who you are, what makes you happy, and what you want from your work life. Losing your job might have been unwelcome and unwarranted, but it wasn't unlucky. It gave you something that you really need: the time to discover your professional self.

After all, how can you write your best résumé, network effectively, interview successfully, negotiate yourself into a new job, or even think about starting your own business if you don't know what you really want? It's a matter of exploring yourself and your options until you find the right fit.

The First Step Forward Is to Look Within

After reading the next several pages, some of you will realize that your current career is perfect for you. If that's the case, then stick with it. After all, you've been fired from your job, not your career.

My guess, however, is that more of you will feel some kind of professional shift is in order. Whether that means doing the same kind of work in a new industry or making an entire career change, as long as the reasons for your move are the right ones, you'll be in good shape.

And lots of valid reasons exist for shifting career gears, many of which you might never even have thought about. I know I hadn't— at least not until I checked with the experts. After consulting with several top-notch career counselors, including Leslie Rose, founder of Career Confidence, Mary Ann Lee, president of WorkPlus, and Gloria Waslyn, an independent career counselor, we came up with the following eleven indicators that signal a career assessment is in order:

(1) PASSION

You've been haunted for years by a particular passion—to care for animals, join a theater group, design jewelry, work with children. Maybe now is the time to explore it. Even if your exploration turns out to be a bust, at least it will have helped you identify those aspects of the field you liked best, which, in turn, could lead you to the *right* career choice.

teaching
musical
groups,
Teaching

(2) OBSOLETE INDUSTRY

What if your entire field is being relegated to the status of the Tyrannosaurus Rex? Michelle, a WIN Workshop graduate, confronted this dilemma. She'd worked for one of the large home sewing pattern companies, but because many women stopped making their own clothes, business fell off, and she was fired along with almost all her co-workers. Since all the other pattern companies were experiencing the same downturn, it made no sense to turn to a competing firm. So she's been spending her time searching for a brand-new career.

(3) BURNOUT

You've been a social worker (or nurse, insurance saleswoman, account executive, commodities trader, etc.) for twenty years and find you just can't muster up the energy and commitment that used to spur you on. Switching companies probably won't help nearly as much as considering an entirely new and revitalizing career option.

(4) RUSTOUT

You're not exactly burned out, but you're pretty bored with your current job function. It's probably time to move in a new direction.

As I once heard Wendy Reid Crisp, national director of NAFE, say, "If you're coasting at your job, you're actually going downhill."

(5) MONEY

I know, I know. Everybody's always told you never to take a job solely for the money. And that's true, but the important word here is "solely," not "money." If you're in a field that lacks decent salaries (whatever "decent" may mean to you), and your resentment is making you miserable, it's a good reason to hunt about for something else.

(6) PERSONAL COST

Sometimes, especially if you've been at a career for several years, you may begin to resent the price you have to pay for holding your position. Maybe the hours are overlong, or there's too much travel—exciting at first, but, for many, wearing over the long run. Whatever the situation, when the personal cost of the job outweighs the benefits, it's time to rethink your options.

(7) UN-SYNC-ABLE VALUES

When your values aren't in sync with those of your company, profession, or industry, you need to reassess your career choice. That's what Linda did. She had a public relations job lots of people would envy: meeting interesting people, attending glamorous parties, and demanding a pretty hefty salary to boot. One thought always nagged at her, though: although there was a lot of sizzle to her work, she felt it lacked "substance." She didn't believe that promoting products and people was a "legitimate" way to use her talents and energy. Now she's looking at a new industry—health communications—which she believes will better suit her values and beliefs.

(8) BAD FIT

It's possible that you're the square peg in your industry's round hole. It's not just your values that don't fit, but your talents or even goals. When there's no place in your current line of work for someone with your particular constellation of skills, interests, enthusiasms, and dreams, do yourself a favor and consider moving on.

(9) OVERPROMOTION

Can't imagine a workplace scenario where you've gotten too many promotions? Carla can. She was a wonderful business reporter—so wonderful, in fact, that after a few years she was named associate editor, then senior editor, and finally editor-in-chief of a national trade magazine. Yet Carla isn't happy: Her passion was writing, and in her high-level position she's spending *all* her time managing staff and overseeing the magazine. She no longer has time to write. So now she's trying to identify a field outside of magazine publishing that will allow her to write and retain the kind of salary and professional status she deserves.

(10) CHANGED ECONOMIC DEMANDS

Maybe you don't have the financial obligations you used to have. For instance, when you were divorced, and your daughter was entering college, you stuck with an unsatisfying but high-paying position to bring in enough money. But now that you've remarried and your daughter has graduated, you may not need a hefty income—or the kind of job that commands it, either.

This works the other way around too. Working as a saleswoman at the local department store may have been fine when you were young, single, and had few financial responsibilities. But now that you have a young child to raise and an elderly parent to care for, you need to put your skills to work in a position in an industry that offers an opportunity to bolster your salary.

(11) YOU'VE BEEN FIRED

The very fact that you've been fired may be a signal that you need to reassess your career choices, because it's quite possible that YOU might have contributed to your current unemployment predicament by taking a position for which you were not suited in the first place. Let me explain.

Suppose you're the kind of person that needs plenty of lead time to do your work. You panic under tight deadlines and can't get the job done well under such pressure. But since your last position was filled with eleventh-hour deadlines, naturally, you didn't shine. You felt inadequate, and it showed.

My advice to you now is this: Scrutinize, honestly and carefully, why you got fired. You'll probably learn some valuable information about yourself that will stop you from making the same mistake twice.

All the Wrong Reasons

This last point brings me to another: It's just as important to understand the wrong reasons for deciding to revamp your career as it is to understand the right ones.

You'll waste a lot of time and energy diving headlong into a new career for a silly reason—like a quick fix for a just-fired and badly bruised ego. If you boomerang into a new position just to show up your ex-boss, and don't give the matter careful thought, chances are you'll move into something that's really not your style. As a result, your days there will probably be numbered.

Lots of other wrong reasons nudge women into trying to redirect their careers. These are some of them:

• Eyeing with envy your friends' fabulous, profitable careers, without giving any thought to the day-by-day activities that define them.

• Entering a field because it's what your father, mother, sister, brother, or aunt does. The corollary of this rotten reason: moving into the family business *solely* because it's the family business.

• Confusing the people at your old company, or the company itself, with an entire industry. Just because your ex-boss or former colleagues were dorks, or the firm was inefficiently run, doesn't mean it's endemic to the industry. Changing fields requires a lot of energy, time, commitment, and plain old hard work, so before you make any major switch, research the new industry to make sure it's where you belong.

• Hearing that a certain career is a growing field, but ignoring the fact that if it doesn't fit your needs, goals, and style, it probably won't be growing with you.

• Going into a field where job security is the *only* plus.

• Repositioning yourself in a new industry *only* because it's a "good field for a woman" (a prime motivation for many teachers, saleswomen, and fashion designers, to name a few).

• Wanting to meet men. No kidding. There are still women out there who go into medicine to meet doctors, into law to meet attorneys, and so forth. Who says we've come a long way?

Each one of these is an awful reason to change your career focus, and if any one of them is yours, I urge you to reconsider. You'll only be trading in your old problems for new ones, something you want to avoid at all costs.

Finding Your Best Self

Now let's go back to that list of valid career assessment indicators. How many items on that list struck a responsive chord? If even one did, then you need to do some hard, clear thinking about your career focus. Here's your objective: to find the position or career that makes you look forward to Monday morning more than Friday afternoon and lights up your face every time you talk about it. Nothing short of that is good enough for you.

You've already taken the first step toward landing a terrific new position by beginning to reevaluate whether you're on the right career path and whether a change of direction is in order. The next step will be even more revealing and valuable, not to mention a lot more fun. It centers on incorporating the best parts of yourself and the things you love the most into your work life.

CAREER ASSESSMENT WORKOUT

Okay, I admit it. I own a workout tape, but I never play it. So I've come up with this no-sweat exercise that even I enjoy. All you have to do is lift a pencil and stretch your imagination.

Ready? Just write down your answer to the following question. (The only rule is not to edit your thoughts or feelings. Write whatever comes to mind as quickly and in as much detail as possible.)

QUESTION: *If you absolutely knew you couldn't fail in your next career move, what would you do?*
Give as many details as you can, including the kind of business you are in, who you work with, what your surroundings are like, the geographical location (near water, a major city), the highlights of a typical day, what you usually wear to work, and whatever else pops into your head.

To give you an idea of how this works, here's how Laura, a recent firee but former vice president of sales for a restaurant supply company, answered:

"I would start a new mail-order catalog called PASSPORT. I would travel the world with a team of buyers, seeking out wonderful gift items to buy. Mostly household goods, but it could also include great wrapping papers, children's books, whatever. I would be responsible for the contents. The buyers would take care of all the paperwork, shipping instructions, and any other follow-up work.

"While we were in each new town, village, or city, I would take time out to walk around, discover, and photograph the local scenery and craftsmen to use as visuals for the catalog.

"Back home at corporate headquarters, high above the city's skyline, I would work with my staff to make sure the catalog came out on time. Quality and unique finds would be the hallmarks of PASSPORT. I would have the final say on all pages for content and style. All the people who worked for PASSPORT would be bright, creative, and care about the company's success. It would also succeed because the mailing list would eventually be filled with people with my taste, waiting for the next catalog.

"Personally, I would have a fabulous wardrobe filled with things I picked up on my travels. I would live in a sensational penthouse in New York City, which I could easily afford thanks to all the money I make from PASSPORT."

Now you try it.

ANALYZING THE NO-FAIL FANTASY

Whether or not you ever realize your no-fail fantasy doesn't matter. What is essential, however, is that you identify those elements of it that are most important to you and try to incorporate them into your next position.

Let's look at Laura's fantasy. Obviously, she loves to travel and shop. But when you probe a little deeper, she also emerges as someone who needs to be in charge. She has to see a project through from beginning to end, although she wants nothing to do with details. Laura also loves to work with things that stimulate her visually—interesting objects, glamorous surroundings, great photographs—even a well-designed catalog. What's more, she has a strong sense of personal style that must be allowed to express itself in everything she does. Finally, Laura wants to surround herself with creative people who, like herself, are devoted to the company.

Now, take a look at what you wrote and spend a few moments exploring what your words say about who you are and what you want. It often helps to show your notes to a trusted friend or colleague who has a more objective viewpoint and can offer another perspective.

By the way, some women find it helps to do the no-fail fantasy exercise more than once, because when they're in different moods, or at a different time and place, they come up with different answers. If you want to give it a few more tries, go ahead. Then where you're done, see if you can find a pattern running through all your fantasies—*that's* the element to which you must pay closest attention. Next, ask yourself these two questions and write down the answers on a separate sheet of paper:

(1) What elements do you have in your no-fail fantasy that you didn't have in your last job? (For example: travel, big salary, impressive title, lots of power, opportunity to work with famous people, fans and adulation.)

(2) Of all of those, which one or two do you feel you *must* have in order to be happy in your next position? (Put a star next to each; these are your "core elements.")

Before you analyze what you starred, a word about what you didn't. Realistically, you probably won't be able to incorporate *all* of the things you fantasized about into your work life. But that's okay. Your career is (or at least should be) just one aspect of a healthy, balanced life. Outside the office, your family, friends, and hobbies can fulfill your other needs and enable you to enjoy your other interests.

Remember Laura? She didn't star this, but part of her fantasy was to photograph all the wonderful places she visited. When she thought about it, though, she realized that that didn't mean that she had to go off and find a job that incorporates photography. She could easily fulfill that need with weekend photo jaunts or by joining a local photography club. As far as her desire to travel internationally (also not starred), she decided that she didn't need to do that as part of her job; instead, that desire could be satisfied with something many career women forget—vacations!

Now, take another look at those core elements you starred and ask yourself this: Is there any way I could interpret those critical elements differently?

Suppose that you starred "having lots of fans and adulation." You might be happy in a position that came with the opportunity for recognition by your boss or your industry for a job well done. On the other hand, you might need to work in a high-profile job in which you are often interviewed by the trade press or asked to speak at professional meetings. Or you might even want a job that would allow you to take center stage at company or industry functions.

Here's another example. Say you starred "working with famous people." First, you have to spell out what you mean by "famous." Do you mean glamorous-famous like Cher, political-famous like Henry Kissinger, business-famous like Lee Iacocca, or perhaps sports-famous like Dorothy Hamill? Now, suppose you mean business-famous. If you think about this further, you may realize that what you really want is to be affiliated with a well-known and well-respected company or businessperson. Or perhaps it means that you would like to work with a product that you feel has great visibility—something like Coca-Cola. In either case, you'll be "famous" by association. Get the idea?

Great. Because once you identify and start to understand your "core elements," you've taken a giant step in finding a position or career that will be a rich source of inspiration and challenge.

That's what happened to Laura. After a good deal of soul-searching, followed by a little preliminary research, she realized that several career paths might be open to her. Among them: (1) working in a marketing or product-development department for an upscale consumer product catalog company; (2) staying in sales but moving to a giftware, jewelry, or home furnishings firm; or (3) managing an organization that produces national or even international trade shows for such creative product lines as toys, gourmet foods, giftware, or stationery.

But we're jumping slightly ahead here. Right now, your next move is to figure out your work style and identify the kind of workplace environment that both fits that style and enables you to put your core elements (and perhaps a few of the other things you fantasized about) into play.

The Road to Success
Is Always Under Construction

The road to success is always under construction. I wish I'd said that, but unfortunately, I didn't—so whoever did, thanks. It's a great line that makes an important point—there are lots of obstacles and detours on a career path and your success lies in being able to navigate them.

One common roadblock is having a work style that doesn't mesh with that of your position, company, or industry. To avoid it, you first need to analyze your own personal work style.

WORK STYLE EXERCISE

Circle or highlight the sentence in each pair that best describes you:

1. I prefer to work in a large, organized corporation.
   I prefer to work in a small, privately owned firm.

2. I need to be in charge.
   I prefer to follow someone else's direction.

3. The idea of a start-up situation excites me.
   I want everything to be in place when I begin.

4. I thrive on constant deadlines and a pressure-cooker atmosphere.
   I'm most productive in a relaxed environment.

5. I prefer to work alone.
   I prefer to be involved in a team effort.

6. I need recognition for my work.
   Self-satisfaction is enough for me.

7. I prefer to work in a big city.
   A suburban or rural setting appeals to me most.

8. A high salary makes me feel most successful.
   A sense of pride in my work makes me feel most successful.

9. I like my days structured and well-planned.
   I prefer days filled with unexpected events.

10. I like working in the office every day.
    I need a periodic change of environment.

11. I feel most comfortable conforming to a corporate dress code.
    I need to convey a more personalized sense of style.

12. I consider myself very creative.
    I'm detail-oriented and methodical.

13. I prefer to share an office.
    I need my own private work space.

14. I can happily conform to company hours.
    I must listen to my own personal clock.

15. I constantly need to learn new things.
    I'm happiest working at things I already know well.

16. I need decisions to be made quickly.
    I understand and can tolerate corporate bureaucracy.

17. I need to see a project through from beginning to end.
    I'm satisfied to do only my part in a project and then let go.

18. I need to see a concrete result of my efforts (such as a published article or a new product).
    I get great satisfaction from intangible results (such as knowing I've taught someone an important skill).

19. I prefer to travel for my job.
    I prefer to stick to home base.

20. I love to meet and work with new people.
    Meeting and working with new people makes me anxious.

Now, take a close look at the statements you've circled. Do your work style preferences match your last working situation?

If most of them do, consider yourself fortunate. Obviously, you were in a professional environment that suited your particular work style. Your job now is to try to keep as many of those elements in your next position as possible. And, if you felt emotionally satisfied in your last job—refer to those "core emotional elements" we discussed earlier—your next move may be as simple as landing another job in a similar company. If so, you have my permission to move on to chapter 6 to start working on your résumé.

More than likely, though, you've completed this exercise and realized that there was a lot of incompatibility between your work style and your former work situation. Further, you've probably discovered that your previous position didn't include those core emotional elements so necessary to your career satisfaction. If that's the case, job-hopping to the same kind of company you just left won't help. You may well need a full-blown career makeover.

Now, before you short-circuit—I admit that last statement can be pretty intimidating—let me say this about career change: *You can do it.* I did, my coauthor did, and so did many of the women who've gone through WIN Workshops. Why, you've already begun your career overhaul by understanding what you need in your next position to get you grinning while you're *at* the office, not just when you leave it!

But whether your career calls for a fine-tuning, a more substantial shift, or an entire overhaul, there's still more work to be done. Realistically, it can take months to make any kind of professional move. But once you've decided what it is you want, you owe it to yourself to go for it. (I never said it would be easy, just productive and very, very important.)

DO YOU NEED AN INTERIM JOB?

As I well know, money is often an overriding concern. Unemployment, even when combined with severance, may be inadequate to keep you afloat. If that's the case for you, then without losing sight of your ultimate (long-term) objective, you also need to concentrate on a more immediate (short-term) goal: replacing your previous job in order to pay your bills and subsidize your career change. A smart move would be to take a position that's less challenging than your last one, even if it offers less pay. Remember, you're no longer trying to make points in the industry or move up the corporate ladder. Instead, you're trying to find a way to survive until you can land the position you want in a field that excites you.

To accomplish this short-term objective, it's probably best to stick to the industry you just left because:

(1) You have the greatest number of contacts there;
(2) Thanks to your experience, your dollar worth is highest there;

(3) You'll interview better because you already know the lingo, as well as industry issues of concern to a potential employer;

(4) Once you land the job, you'll feel relatively comfortable because you're familiar with the industry turf;

(5) Since you know what you're doing, and won't be totally drained in learning a whole new field, you should have the time and energy to explore your future career.

The skills required to find this interim position are the same ones you'll need to change careers—résumé writing, networking, interviewing, and negotiating. So as you read the remaining chapters, keep both your long- and short-term objectives in mind.

Ten Sound Strategies for Career Change

If you want to embark on a completely new career path, you need to follow some sound career-change strategies. Here are the ten I recommend:

STRATEGY NUMBER ONE:
EXPLORE YOUR FANTASY

Hooray! You've already begun this by completing the previous exercises. (You did do them, didn't you?) You've fantasized about your dream career, discovered your work style, and, in the process, learned a lot about yourself. Keep this information in mind as you move along.

STRATEGY NUMBER TWO:
CONSTRUCT TWO SKILLS LISTS

I'm a big one for making lists, probably because I have so many things on my mind all the time that I find it an easy way to get organized. So take out another piece of paper and construct two lists.

The first is a list of those skills you used on your last job. To construct this list, break your job down into all of its various segments in as much detail as possible.

Here's a hypothetical sample from a national sales manager in an office supply company.

- Called on key accounts nationally.
- Cold-called for new business, East Coast only.
- Worked with marketing department to produce company catalog and direct-mail pieces.
- Kept in touch weekly with national sales force of twelve.
- Hired and fired salespersons.
- Trained sales staff.
- Projected annual sales.
- Organized annual sales meeting (contacted hotels, arranged rooms, rented video equipment, booked guest speaker).
- Handled difficult customer complaints that other salespersons could not, such as short-shipping, nonshipment, damaged merchandise, returns.
- Organized participation in six annual trade shows (hired models to distribute literature, worked with design team for booth displays, negotiated location and cost of booths).
- Traveled nationally on goodwill trips to meet with key accounts.

The idea here is to dissect your day-to-day activities. A good way to get started is to pull out your résumé and/or former job description and see what phrases pop out at you. (Once you're done constructing this list, save it. We'll use it later on in another chapter.)

Now we're going to create another list. For this one, detail those skills you possess but have never gotten a chance to use in your work. For example, you're a terrific public speaker but have never done it on the job, or you always sell the most raffle tickets at the community center but you've never been in a position to show off your sales skills at the office. So your list might look something like this:

- Public speaking.
- Selling.
- Creating community fund-raising ideas/events.
- Speaking French fluently.
- Refinishing antique furniture.
- Filming and editing home videos.
- Breeding and showing Shih-Tzus.

Next, take these two lists and put a check beside those skills that give you the most satisfaction. This skills profile will help you paint an even clearer picture of the elements you need to incorporate into your next position.

STRATEGY NUMBER THREE:
NAME THAT POSITION

Now that you know what you really would want in the best of all worlds—what fits your style, what skills you have and which you enjoy—you need to identify those careers and fields that can give you most of what you need. Notice I said "*most*." As I mentioned before, in the real world it's hard to find a career with no downsides at all. Still, you can get pretty darn close if you concentrate on the task at hand—finding out who gets paid to do the kinds of things you love to do.

The way to do this is by talking to as many people as you can; describing, in as much detail as possible, what you want to do; and asking them, "Who earns a living doing it?" You may even discover a career option that you hadn't known existed. Try this one-on-one, or, if you like, in a group brainstorming session. (You may also consider seeking out a professional career consultant; but this can be a very expensive option.)

During one WIN Workshop, for example, Eileen said she wanted to work with people, to be involved with a project all the way through, to play detective and track down new resources or suppliers for goods or services, and, if possible, to be surrounded by her passion—exotic flowers. She also said she preferred to work either on her own or with only one or two other professionals. How's that for a mixed bag of desires?

But the workshop group was not daunted. Within a short time, they came up with several suggestions. The one that immediately intrigued Eileen was becoming a wedding planner and consultant— a career she had never heard of before. It fit her perfectly, right down to her love of flowers. See how this can work?

Consider one more idea. Remember when I talked about why women are more vulnerable to getting fired than men? One of the reasons was that women tend to take staff positions in advertising, personnel, marketing, and other fields rather than in areas with bottom-line responsibility. Well, that doesn't have to be the case for- ever. If you have a real interest or ability in such areas as finance, production, or sales, don't dismiss these possible career options. True, they're dominated by men, but women can and have made in- roads. I'm not telling you to pursue these avenues solely because they'll give you more protection against being fired, although, admittedly, they probably will. Just don't eliminate them if they appeal to you.

STRATEGY NUMBER FOUR:
GET THEE TO A LIBRARY

Once you have a pretty good idea of which fields or careers may work best for you, learn more about them. A good place to begin your research is the library. There's got to be a book, trade magazine, or at least an article or two on nearly every career you could think of, lists of associations and organizations to help you network in these fields, as well as a few dozen books that go into great detail on how to change careers. (If you haven't read it yet, do pick up a copy of *What Color Is Your Parachute?*—in my opinion, one of the best and most popular guides to career change. Another excellent publication is *Wishcraft*; check out the resource section at the end of this book for information on these and other selections.)

STRATEGY NUMBER FIVE:
NETWORK YOUR NET WORTH

Meet and talk to whomever you can—that's the cardinal rule of networking. Speaking with as many people as possible in the fields you're interested in, as well as individuals in other fields, may lead you to all sorts of new opportunities.

Another plus of networking before making a career change: It lets you test the waters without getting soaked. Speaking with people who are already doing what you think you want to do—and finding out many of the everyday details on the job, including perks and pitfalls—will help you decide whether this field is for you. (I'll discuss networking in greater detail in chapter 7.)

STRATEGY NUMBER SIX:
TAKE ADVANTAGE OF ONE-NIGHT STANDS

Bet you never thought you'd be reading about one-night stands in a woman's business advice book, but actually I believe they're a wonderful way to sample a new career. If you know the right kind of one-nighter to indulge in, that is. The kind I'm talking about is offered by Y's, community centers, and continuing education institutions: inexpensive, one-night seminars or lectures that give you a bite-size chunk of a particular career. They are usually taught by experts in the field and can be a wonderful source of quick, intensive information. Plus, they provide another opportunity for you to network with someone about your new field or interest.

STRATEGY NUMBER SEVEN:
CREATE A CAREER COLLAGE

Career counselor Leslie Rose told me about a terrific way to sample several fields of interest at the same time: create a collage of part-time positions. For example, a former office manager toying with the idea of starting her own business—either going into the food service industry or working with children—might start an at-home typing service in the mornings (to ensure that she can pay the bills), assist a gourmet catering concern at night, and cater and organize children's parties on Saturday afternoons. After several months, she may have a clearer picture of what it is she really wants.

STRATEGY NUMBER EIGHT:
BACK TO SCHOOL

Some careers demand your going back to school. If you want to be a lawyer, psychologist, real estate broker, or veterinarian, you can do all the networking in the world but you won't be able to practice legally until you get the education and certification. So before you invest time and money—and you can be talking BIG money and LOTS of time here—to further your education, make sure you understand exactly what this new field entails: Talk with other professionals, hang around while they work, volunteer in the field, and read the professional magazines and journals.

STRATEGY NUMBER NINE:
LEARN STRATEGIC MARKETING

Once you've decided on a career, you need to present yourself as someone who fits the needs of that new field. Ann Hunt, vice president and partner at Korn/Ferry International, one of the largest executive search firms in the world, says that it's all a matter of marketing. She's seen several career changers get great jobs, even be recruited for them, from outside of their fields.

"Today," says Hunt, "companies are willing to take a chance on career changers, particularly if you've marketed yourself for a strategic hire." That is, explains Hunt, "a company may have a strategic reason for needing a specific kind of individual—say they need an executive with a track record for turning a floundering company around. If you can market yourself with that company's needs in mind, you may be a good candidate. For example, you have a background in marketing and you were brought into XYZ Cosmetics when the CEO there realized he needed to develop and market products for older women. You did a wonderful job for that company and attracted millions of fifty-plus female consumers. Then you can say, 'Well, XYZ Bank, I can do the same for you.'"

STRATEGY NUMBER TEN:
PACKAGE A POSITION

It may be that after you've identified a field and what you'd like to do in it, you cannot find any position that offers you what you want. Maybe that position simply does not exist.

Don't despair. This is a fabulous opportunity! You may be able to create your own job and pitch it to a corporation with the budget to hire you. In corporate lingo, it's called "adding a new dimension to an existing service," but in plain English it means a great deal for you!

I know of a woman who wanted to bring medical self-awareness to the general public. She couldn't find a company that had a job that fit this description, so she put together a proposal and pitched it to Blue Cross/Blue Shield, which loved the idea and created a job for her. Now she has a wonderful career doing videos and seminars for companies on such topics as quitting smoking and learning how to relax.

They Did It!
Real-Life Career Changers

These strategies work. I know because I've seen them work. For real live women, in real-life situations. Take Bobbi Van, for instance.

THE QUEEN OF CAREER CHANGE

I call Bobbi the queen of career change because she's done it so often and so very, very successfully. For ten years she sold advertising space for major newsstand magazines. Then, thanks to office politics, she was fired.

Bobbi was devastated. "I felt like I had lost my identity, like I was being punished. But you know the expression 'When a window closes, a door opens'? It's true. Getting fired turned out to be the best thing that ever happened to me." (Now where have you heard *that* before? Beginning to believe it?)

Soon after she started job hunting, she had an offer to work for *National Lampoon* for "an excellent promotional guy there. But I thought that I should try to stick with sales and with a larger company. One morning, I had an interview at a big corporate publishing firm, but as I stood outside the building, I started to cry. It suddenly hit me that I didn't want to go that route again. So there I was, standing outside this huge office building and crying, when a business friend of mine came along. When I told him what was wrong, he encouraged me to take the *National Lampoon* offer. I did, stayed there one year and learned a lot, then left for an opportunity to co-produce the *People* magazine parody."

Meanwhile, Bobbi had developed an interest in video production and making documentaries. Saving her money while learning more about the field—mostly by taking video courses—she decided to strike out on her own and launch a video production company. "I went for broke; hired a public relations firm, got enormous amounts of publicity, and produced a documentary called *To Bear Witness*, now in a New York museum." But the real money came when individuals hired Bobbi's company to tell their life stories on videotape.

"My business became very lucrative from these video biographies, but I soon realized that documentaries were where I got the most satisfaction, and unfortunately, there was not much money to be made from them. So, I began researching business trends and discovered that I liked the promotional area." Making some key contacts through networking, Bobbi and a partner launched their own company specializing in corporate gifts and incentives.

"We worked every day till ten or eleven P.M. and learned a lot about the business on the job. It was the most exciting time of my life." It paid off in other ways too—by the third year, the firm was grossing over $1 million.

For six years Bobbi worked at her business. But then burnout set in. "I started to reassess and finally decided to sell the company." Today, she's recharging herself while considering new business opportunities.

SELF-MAID WOMAN

Gina was earning $40,000 annually as the corporate information manager for a luxury car manufacturer when sex discrimination caused her to lose her job. "I was so angry; I felt my integrity as a person had been violated. I had given that job *everything*. I felt I had hit rock bottom."

Then Gina did something very interesting. "At the point when I just didn't care if I ever got another job, I started thinking about law school. I had started studying once when I was much younger, but had to quit due to finances. I still had no money but now it didn't seem to matter. My situation couldn't get any worse. So I applied and was accepted to law school."

It wasn't easy, but Gina was determined. Working as a maid, cleaning houses seven days a week and taking classes at night for three and a half years, Gina finally got her law degree. She passed the bar in 1987 and is now in private practice specializing in family law and immigration. And in retrospect, she says getting fired helped her get where she is today.

"When you're tied to the umbilical cord of salary checks and employee benefits you don't take the risks. But when you are fired, you can take the risks and go for it."

OUT OF ACADEMIA

Jean was associate director of admissions at a private college when a change in management forced her out of her job. "I should have seen it coming; the new dean had already let the rest of the department go. But somehow I didn't, so when he fired me, I was shocked and very angry." Eventually, though, Jean managed to find another job heading up an educational program for adults.

"While I was there, I started realizing that I'd probably have more opportunities, financially and otherwise, in the business world. At the same time, I became friendly with the school's corporate relations officer, who encouraged me to try her field, fund-raising. So, when she left her job, I applied—and got it."

Although still in academia, Jean was now involved with the business side of things. She helped raise scholarship money, solicited funds for special programs, and helped the school establish closer ties with the business community. Things were going smoothly when the boss she loved left and was replaced by "a woman who did not like me at all." This time, however, she "didn't want to be fired."

Emphasizing her fund-raising experience, Jean began networking. Through a friend in the field, she landed several interviews and eventually was hired as the director of development for a national Jewish fund-raising organization. Her move out of academia and into fund-raising was complete.

One Last Word on Career Change

I hope that many of you have now discovered that you have what it takes to make an exciting career change. But others of you may be saying, "I'm not feeling very hopeful or confident or positive right now. Does that mean that career change is out of the question?"

NO WAY! Anyone can successfully change or revamp her career if she sets her mind to it. And now you've got a jump on the whole process. But if you don't feel completely ready to take action, don't get discouraged. It may mean that for a while, at least until your confidence and courage return, you'll need to work a little more at considering your options.

But once you've got a fix on what your next career move should be—whether that's merely replacing your former job or striking out in an entirely new direction—you can start to write an effective résumé.

6.

Résumés: All the You That's Fit to Print

One of the questions I'm asked most frequently is how to write an effective résumé. Some women have never written one, mostly because they felt they never needed to. I know that was the case for me. In the close-knit apparel industry, I had always been able to land new positions by networking, until I lost my last job and the market was so depressed that networking alone was not enough. Let's face it, though, even if you may think you're "above" needing a résumé, as I thought I was, there will be times when your job search will demand it. If you already have a résumé, you're one step ahead of the game, but even so, it could probably stand some updating and improvement.

Unfortunately, though, the easiest time to write an effective résumé is when you're still working; that's when you're most tuned in to your skills and most confident in your abilities. Once you're out of work, your tendency is to question your worth and forget your accomplishments.

Yet now is an opportune time to sit down and put together a powerful résumé. After all, you've got a few extra hours on your hands. You've also got some pretty important motivation—you need another job! Well, a good résumé will help you get it.

What's more, writing (or rewriting) your résumé is a wonderful morale booster. It gives you the opportunity to spend some time thinking about all the things you've accomplished and how successful you've really been. Soon you'll start hearing yourself say, "Right! I *did* run the sales meeting all by myself. I *was* responsible for bringing in four new accounts this year, and I *was* the one who instituted a successful company newsletter." It's amazing what a quick pick-me-up these recollections can be!

Now, I know that lots of books already exist on how to write a résumé. But have you ever read them carefully? Almost all are written *by* men and are primarily *for* men. Generally, they include training and career histories comprised of such entries as chemical engineer or national sales manager for an industrial machinery manufacturer. Not exactly fields filled with women or résumés written in language you'll find useful.

My intention is to remedy this situation by addressing your needs more particularly in this chapter. First, I'll answer the ten questions women most often ask about résumés and offer additional tips. Second, I'll show you samples of other women's efforts that will serve as more appropriate models for writing your most effective résumé.

Emily's Top Ten Questions About Résumés

(1) IS A TWO-PAGE RÉSUMÉ ACCEPTABLE?

The average résumé has between 20 and 30 seconds to make its first impression. In that time, the reader will skim it to find out which companies you've worked for, what your positions were, how long you worked at each firm, and, perhaps, where and when you went to school. Remember, a résumé is a summation of the high points, not your life story, which is why most experts say one-page résumés are preferable.

If, however, your career history is so diverse and/or extensive that one page won't do it justice, then by all means use an additional page. If you choose to use two pages, though, make sure to put your *full name*, plus the page number, at the top of the second page, and staple both sheets together so that they don't come apart. Use a paper clip to attach your cover letter and business card to your résumé; never use staples here.

Here's another tip: Leave some things off your résumé. I know this sounds peculiar—I know because my collaborator just said, "This sounds peculiar"—but let me explain. If your résumé highlights all of your accomplishments, it leaves nothing new for you to talk about in an interview or mention in a cover letter. For those times, hold back one or two points that won't detract from your résumé's effectiveness. Two examples: (1) when your boss was on a three-month maternity leave you ran the department, or (2) because you are bilingual, you were often called upon to act as a hostess for your company's foreign clients.

(2) HOW MANY REFERENCES SHOULD I LIST?

None. That's right, zero. You should provide references only during an interview when and if a potential employer requests them. You'll find it helpful, however, to prepare a typed list of references to leave with the interviewer if he or she requests them. Include three to seven names, with each entry's title, company, and phone number.

Some professional résumé writers suggest putting "References available upon request" at the end of your résumé, but I feel it's unnecessary—*of course* you'll provide references if you're asked. If, however, sticking to the "standard" form makes you feel better, you won't lose any points for it.

(3) SHOULD I LIST A SHORT-TERM JOB?

That depends on your definition of short-term. I would say that if you were at most of your positions for more than two years, and only one or two others for less than six months (many of us have had that experience once in our careers), I would omit the short-term positions and be a little creative with the dates for the longer jobs.

For example, suppose you worked at Avalon Agency from May 1972 to November 1976. Then you made a mistake and went to the Biltmore Agency, where you lasted only four months, until March of 1977. Your next position, at the Carlyle Agency, began in May of 1977 and you worked there till December of 1982.

Your résumé should read:
    1972–1976 Avalon agency
    1977–1982 Carlyle Agency

By omitting the months, you've eliminated a lot of unnecessary questions. (For more on "creative dating," see the special tips section later in this chapter.)

You should only include a short-term job on your résumé if it will enhance your professional image and if the reason you stayed there for a short time is easily explained. A good example would be if you went to work for a very prestigious company on a project basis, knowing in advance that the job would last for a specific time period. In that case, you would name the company, the length of the project, and your accomplishments.

(4) SHOULD I INCLUDE PERSONAL INFORMATION SUCH AS (A) MARITAL STATUS (B) HEALTH, OR (C) HOBBIES?

(a) Absolutely not. (b) Absolutely not. (c) Well, maybe.

Your marital status is no one's business. The main reason employers want to know about it is to gauge whether or not you have (or might be having) children and whether you'll need time off from, or are likely to quit, work. Your health is solely your business, too.

You are under no obligation either on your résumé or in an interview to divulge such personal information.

Hobbies are another story. My rule of thumb is to include them only if they'll make you sound so fascinating that prospective employers will have to interview you. But even when your hobbies are provocative—for instance, you have a pilot's license, you act in a local repertory theater, or you breed champion Dalmations—you run a risk of alienating a potential boss who gets airsick at the very thought of flying, believes all actors are flakes, or is allergic to dogs. It's your call here, but if it were me, I'd leave them out.

(5) SHOULD I INCLUDE MY AGE?

A lot of women who are 40 and over omit the date of their college graduation as well as their first job or two in an attempt to appear younger on paper. One older woman I know went so far as to leave the entire first part of her career off her résumé. But that made it look as if her first job had been vice president of a major office supply company. Pretty good for a job right out of college!

I believe that if you leave such important information off your résumé you just send up a flare that you're trying to cover up something. Even if you can get away with it on paper, you're not going to get away with it in person. I also feel that if a company is not going to interview you because of your age, then it's probably not the right company for you anyway.

(6) HOW DO I HANDLE MY FIRING IN PRINT?

List your most recent position with a start date and leave it open-ended. This way, it will look as if you wrote the résumé while you were still working (which is when you should have written it, anyway). Even if you're out of work several months, that's okay. Just say that this is your most recent résumé, which is true. There's no reason to include your firing date anywhere.

(7) WHAT PAPER, COLOR, AND TYPEFACE SHOULD I USE?

When it comes to paper stock, there's just one rule: Go for the best you can afford. Most printers I've spoken with recommend between 20- and 24-pound paper.

As for color, white, off-white, cream, beige, or pale gray are the most acceptable. Some people think that choosing an offbeat color will help them stand out. They're right, but not in the way they think. Most employers are put off by odd résumé colors, so why take the risk?

Let's consider typeface. In this day and age, many people do their résumés on word processors or computers. This has three main advantages: (1) it's cheaper; (2) it allows the flexibility to change the résumé easily whenever you wish; and (3) it demonstrates that you're computer literate. The disadvantage is that you're often restricted in your choice of typeface, but as long as the computer type is clear and easy to read, feel free to go high-tech. Laser, letter-quality, and twenty-pin dot matrix printers are fine, but avoid the kind of print that *looks* like it came from a computer.

Print out a master copy and take it to a photocopying service that can run off as many copies as you need (twenty or twenty-five is probably adequate) on good paper stock that they or you supply. I went to a local office supply store where the selection of paper was much wider and less expensive. I bought a box of good paper and matching envelopes and had my résumé copied on those.)

If you don't have the option of working on a word processor, want more typefaces to choose from, or are so focused in your job search that one version of your résumé is all you need, then by all means have it professionally printed. Just be prepared to spend a little (well, maybe a lot) more.

If you work with a printer, you'll have more typefaces from which to choose. Helvetica is the most popular because it's simple, clean, readable, and therefore businesslike, so ask to see it. You can opt for another style, but avoid overly graphic and ornate variations.

When choosing a type size, the only criterion is that it be easy to read. Generally 10- and 12-point type are the most useful for the body copy, though you should choose a larger size, ALL CAPS, and/ or **bolder type** for your name and headings. (See the sample résumés at the end of this chapter.)

If you already have a personal business card, you may want to match your résumé to it. If you don't have a business card yet, choose the type style you want and use the opportunity to coordinate both.

Make sure the style of your résumé conforms to the tone of the industry in which you are seeking work. You can be a little more creative, even a bit inventive, if you're seeking a job in the art department of an ad agency than if you're looking for a position with a bank.

(8) CAN AND SHOULD I HAVE MORE THAN ONE RÉSUMÉ?

Yes, you can, and maybe you should. First of all, if you are simultaneously seeking work in two segments of a particular industry, you may want to have two separate résumés, each tailored to a specific position.

You might also need a second—or even a third—résumé if you are looking for a position in more than one industry. Let's say you were a marketing director for a toy company. That still appeals to you, but you always wanted to work for a celebrity public relations company or be a special events coordinator for a major department store. You'll need a second résumé to emphasize those facets of your background that would best apply to the particular position.

If you're considering a career change, you may want to write a functional, as opposed to the more common chronological, résumé. Most of us are already familiar with a chronological resume; that is, work experience arranged in reverse time sequence. A functional résumé catalogs your work history and abilities by major areas of expertise such as sales, marketing, administration, or finance. (See the résumés at the end of this chapter for examples of both.)

(9) SHOULD I INCLUDE A BRIEF PROFILE OR OBJECTIVE AT THE TOP OF MY RÉSUMÉ?

There are different schools of thought on this, but I recommend it simply because it's a good way to convey quickly the image you're trying to project. For instance, if you were the office manager of a local nonprofit organization and part of the job was planning and organizing three major fund-raising events each year—something you'd now like to do full-time—you should include a profile; that is, a brief, one- or two-line description of your professional self, at the top of your résumé. Here's a sample:

> Profile: Nonprofit professional offering ten years' fund-raising experience, with special expertise in planning, organizing, and coordinating publicity for special events.

If you prefer to use an objective—that is, a brief statement of your current career goals—write something like:

> Objective: To find a position as a fund-raiser for a company that will utilize my background and expertise in planning, organizing, and coordinating publicity for special fund-raising events.

Again, if you're writing your résumé on a computer, you have the flexibility to tailor your profile or objective to fit a specific job opening. So by all means, take advantage of it.

(10) DO I NEED A COVER LETTER?

Yes. Always. Résumés offer a structured and formal picture of you. They give all the pertinent information, but they don't allow for much personality to shine through.

A cover letter, on the other hand, gives you the opportunity to present yourself in a more individual way. If written properly, in a concise, simple, and conversational manner, it allows you to catch the reader's attention by personally introducing yourself and explaining how the reader will benefit from meeting you. To accomplish this, you'll need to target each letter to its particular recipient.

Let me give you a few tips on writing an effective cover letter. (For samples, see pages 133–36.)

• If you're responding to a want ad or if someone has referred you to a company for an available job, always make reference to that in the first or second sentence.

• Earlier, I told you to leave a couple of minor but interesting things off your résumé to allow you a strong cover letter and, perhaps, interview. Well, here's where you put them in, in a few brief sentences that comprise the second paragraph. For instance: "When my company's senior vice president was out on a three-month maternity leave this past year, I stepped in and ran her division. My performance during this period led to my promotion to vice president of another division when she returned."

• The third and usually last paragraph lets the reader politely know that *you* will be contacting *him or her* (NOT the other way around) at a specific time in the near future. And do be sure to extend your thanks for the reader's time and attention.

• All cover letters should be typewritten. You may also want to put them on letterhead stationery that matches your résumé and business card for a very professional look. At the very least, use plain white typing paper.

This letter is intended to accompany your résumé; therefore, don't fall into the trap of repeating the information you've detailed there, such as where you went to school or what duties you performed on your last job.

A Few More Pertinent Pointers

I have a few more pointers I want to offer before I show you some good examples of résumés and cover letters:

• Don't include any moonlighting. If you've done free-lance or consulting work while you held a full-time job, even if you were moonlighting for the most prestigious company in your field, DO

NOT include it. You don't want to give the impression that you didn't devote 100 percent of your time and energy to your job. Your potential employers may worry that you'll do the very same thing at their company and that might stop them from hiring you.

As usual, there's an exception to the rule: If free-lance or consulting work *outside your industry* is the best or only credential you have for the position you're shooting for, you may need to include it. Suppose, for example, that you are a banquet manager for a large hotel but your new career objective is to manage, and eventually own, a spa. In that case, you should mention the evenings and weekends you spent managing a local health club in either your cover letter or résumé.

• Don't include months on a résumé when listing dates of employment for each job. As I explained earlier, this serves to flag short-term jobs. Also, if you've ever been pink-slipped before and were out of work for, say, four months, by focusing on years (and omitting months), you can delete your period of unemployment—with no explanation necessary!

• Eliminate repetitions. Sometimes you've held more than one job with the same functions and responsibilities. In that case, explain only the most recent job fully. There's no need to repeat information you've already provided.

• Check-up time. After you write your résumé, but before you have it printed, have a friend or respected colleague (preferably both) critique it for you. An outsider will view your résumé with a fresh perspective and may be able to point out awkward or prejudicial phrases that might undermine its effectiveness.

Pamela, for instance, had owned her own company for several years. After it closed, she took a position working for someone else and was fired. But at that time in her career, she felt it was best to look for another industry position rather than go out on her own again. Yet on her résumé, she described herself as a "natural entrepreneur." She was, after all, proud of the fact that she'd run her own company for nine years. But after I read her résumé, I told her to take out that phrase; the last thing she needed to convey to a prospective employer was that she was an entrepreneur and not a company person. Pamela had been too close to her career to understand what it was she was really communicating.

You may be using too much industry jargon in your résumé to describe what you did and what you're seeking, particularly if you're looking to situate yourself outside of your field. This is especially true if you've been in the same industry for most of your career. So it's particularly important to have a friend outside of your industry go over your résumé to make sure it's clear.

The final reason to have someone else read your résumé is to catch typos. Sylvia, for example, had accidentally transposed two of the numbers in her phone number. She didn't realize it until *after* she had sent off bunches of résumés.

• Use action verbs. Here are two sentences that appeared on real résumés. Which reads better?

Was responsible for starting and putting together a monthly company newsletter or *Initiated and edited company's monthly newsletter.*

How about these? Choose the one that's most appealing.

I changed the way the accounting department was run and brought in new computerized systems or *Restructured accounting department and introduced new computerized systems.*

In each case, the second version is the more interesting and powerful one because it uses lively action verbs, such as "initiated," "edited," "restructured," "introduced," and "coordinated," to describe job functions. These verbs give your résumé a more colorful, participatory feeling—in a nutshell, they make it more readable, potent, and professional.

Take a look at the action verb list I've compiled:

ACTION VERB LIST

accelerated	achieved	arranged
accommodated	administrated	assumed
accomplished	advised	authorized
acclimated	analyzed	broadened
acquired	approved	budgeted

built
capitalized
cataloged
collaborated
completed
compiled
conceived
conducted
contributed
consolidated
contracted
controlled
converted
coordinated
created
decreased
defined
delivered
demonstrated
designed
developed
devised
directed
distributed
doubled
earned
edited
eliminated
enhanced
enlarged
established
expanded
expedited
facilitated
focused
forecast
formulated
founded

generated
governed
grouped
guided
headed
hiked
identified
implemented
improved
improvised
inaugurated
increased
installed
instituted
instructed
insured
interacted
interfaced
intensified
introduced
invented
investigated
launched
led
lessened
maintained
managed
maneuvered
maximized
merged
minimized
moderated
monitored
negotiated
operated
optimized
organized
originated

oversaw
performed
pinpointed
planned
presented
prevented
prioritized
processed
progressed
produced
profiled
profited
programmed
promoted
propelled
proposed
provided
purchased
recognized
recommended
recruited
redesigned
reduced
reorganized
researched
reshaped
restructured
revamped
revised
revitalized
saved
scheduled
serviced
set up
simplified
slashed
sold
solved

sorted	superseded	trimmed
sparked	supervised	tripled
spearheaded	surpassed	uncovered
spurred	systematized	unified
staffed	targeted	unraveled
stabilized	taught	used
started	terminated	utilized
streamlined	traced	vacated
strengthened	tracked	verified
stressed	traded	widened
stretched	trained	withdrew
structured	transferred	won
succeeded	transformed	worked
summarized	translated	wrote

There are two good ways to use this list. The first is to write down each function you performed in your previous jobs, then look at the list and choose the most appropriate action verb to describe them.

The second is to read the list slowly and see if any of the verbs triggers a job function that you might have forgotten. For example, when I came across the word "launched," I remembered that I had launched a new division for my company three years earlier and had completely forgotten about it.

Now that we've discussed résumé and cover letter basics, let's take a look at the "before" and "after" example of an effective résumé, then review several finished résumés of women in various fields.

EXAMPLE #1: CHRONOLOGICAL RÉSUMÉ, "BEFORE"

DIANE BIXBY
210 Hawk Street
Highland Park, IL 60035
(312) 555-1023
⑩

① **PERSONAL:** 5′6″   140 lbs   Divorced

② **EDUCATION:**
B.S. Marketing, Boston University, Boston, MA
M.S. Education, Columbia University, NY, NY

EMPLOYMENT

③ NATIONAL TRUST COMPANY, Chicago, IL
⑤
④ • Vice President, Human Resources   Jan. 1987-
I planned, delivered and coordinated all of the training programs for
a department consisting of 400 people. My responsibilities included the
management and supervision of skills and time management programs,
⑥ as well as motivational techniques. I recruited and interviewed for all
staff positions including department managers. Since the company is
going through a corporate downsizing, I was also responsible for
managing the firm's outplacement program.

⑤
④ • Asst. Vice President, Human Resources   Feb. 1984-Dec. 1986
I hired and worked with all outside consultants for special training
needs of 100 managers. I started a recruiting program for the bank as
⑥ well as a career pathing program. I was also responsible for developing
a training program. In this position, I helped design programs for
interviewing, performance appraisals, counseling and problem solving.

⑤
• Asst. Treasurer, Human Resources Devel. Center   Oct. 1981-
Jan. 1984
I designed and implemented bankwide supervisory and management
programs which included oral presentation skills, conflict management,
⑥ customer service and working with people skills. In addition, I managed
office skills center involving the planning, development, coordination and

administration of bankwide training programs that met skills needs of bank employees.

• Katherine Gibbs School, NY, NY
Senior Instructor/Administrator⑤Sept. 1974-Aug. 1981
I was responsible for designing and instructing curricula in the areas ⑥ of Office Information Systems, Administrative and Secretarial Procedures, Accounting and Typing.

⑦ **Hobbies:** Gourmet cooking, aerobics, photography, reading

⑧ **Professional Affiliations:** Member, Association of Human Resource Professionals, 1982-1986

⑨ References will be furnished upon request.

CORRECTIONS:

(1) Delete personal data.
(2) List education after work experience. List your education first only if you've been out of school five years or less.
(3) Insert start date next to name of company.
(4) Write out title and put in bold type.
(5) Eliminate months.
(6) Change description of most recent position to present tense; tighten and edit copy; use action verbs; break information down into bulleted points.
(7) Delete hobbies.
(8) Delete "Member" and years.
(9) Delete (optional).
(10) Write and insert professional profile.

EXAMPLE #1: CHRONOLOGICAL RÉSUMÉ, "AFTER"

DIANE BIXBY
210 Hawk Street
Highland Park, IL 60035
(312) 555-1023

PROFILE
Human resources professional with over 8 years of progressive and increasing responsibility in a major financial institution. Strong skills in problem-solving, communication, leadership and administration.

PROFESSIONAL EXPERIENCE
NATIONAL TRUST COMPANY, Chicago, IL   1981-

Vice President, Human Resources   1987-
* Plan, deliver and coordinate all training programs for 400-person department.
* Supervise skills, time management and motivational technique programs.
* Recruit and interview all levels of staff.
* Manage outplacement program.

Assistant Vice President, Human Resources   1984–1987
* Negotiated and coordinated with outside consultants for special training needs of 100 managers.
* Developed and implemented recruiting, career pathing and training program.
* Designed and delivered department-specific training programs: Interviewing Techniques, Performance Appraisals, Counseling and Problem-Solving Techniques.

Assistant Treasurer, Human Resource Development Center
1981-1984
* Designed and implemented bankwide supervisory and management programs, including oral presentation skills, conflict management and customer service.

110

- Managed office skills center involving the planning, development, coordination and administration of bankwide training programs.

KATHERINE GIBBS SCHOOL, New York, NY   1974–1981

Senior Instructor/Administrator
- Designed and instructed curricula in Office Information Systems, Administrative and Secretarial Procedures, Accounting and Typing.

EDUCATION
B.S., Marketing, Boston University, Boston, MA 1974
M.S., Education, Columbia University, New York, NY 1972

Professional Affiliations
Association of Human Resource Professionals

EXAMPLE #2: CHRONOLOGICAL RÉSUMÉ

ELEANOR DEMPSEY

70 NEWFIELD AVE.   203 555-0000
STAMFORD, CT 06905

PROFILE   ENTHUSIASTIC PROFESSIONAL WITH 23 YEARS
              EXPERIENCE IN FASHION DESIGN AND
              MERCHANDISING, STRONG MARKETING AND
              MANAGERIAL SKILLS. VERY CREATIVE, WITH
              NATURAL AFFINITY FOR PROMOTION AND PUBLIC
              RELATIONS.

EXPERIENCE:

SMYTH LTD.   **VICE-PRESIDENT MERCHANDISING 1982–**
- RESTRUCTURED COMPANY FROM ''SUZI
  CASUALS''—TRADITIONAL DOUBLE KNIT
  COMPANY TO UP-DATED WOVENS (RESULTING
  IN A 15% INCREASE IN VOLUME THE FIRST
  YEAR).
- INITIATED CHANGE IN COMPANY NAME WHICH
  WOULD EMPHASIZE THE NEW IMAGE. ADDED A
  PETITE DIVISION (FOR THE NEW LABEL) TO THE
  EXISTING MISSY AND LARGE SIZES, AND MOVED
  THE FIT DEPT. FROM THE FACTORY (BOSTON)
  TO N.Y. FOR BETTER CONTROL.
- ESTABLISHED ''EXECUTIVE DRESSING'' IN 1983,
  A SUB-DIVISION UNDER THE SMYTH LTD.
  UMBRELLA. THIS BECAME 25% OF THE ANNUAL
  VOLUME, MAINTAINING MARKET SHARE IN A
  DECLINING DEPARTMENT.

- DEVELOPED PRIVATE LABEL PROGRAMS WITH SEVERAL ACCOUNTS GENERATING APPROXIMATELY $4 MILLION PLUS IN SALES ANNUALLY.
- DIRECT AND OVERSEE EFFORTS OF DESIGN TEAMS FOR ALL DIVISIONS.
- CREATED LAUREN LTD. 1986—AN UPDATED RELATED SEPARATES DIVISION (FIRST YEAR APPROXIMATELY $2.5 MILLION IN SALES).
- ORGANIZE AND RUN FOUR NATIONAL SALES MEETINGS PER YEAR.
- WORK WITH IN-HOUSE ADVERTISING DEPARTMENT (ON LOGOS, NATIONAL ADS, PROMOTIONAL MAILERS, ETC.).
- SHOP EUROPEAN MARKETS AND FABRIC SHOWS, AND WORK DIRECTLY WITH ITALIAN MILLS TO DEVELOP NEW PRODUCTS.
- TRAVEL DOMESTICALLY TO WORK WITH MAJOR ACCOUNTS.
- ATTEND QUARTERLY BOARD MEETINGS (AS AN OFFICER ON THE OPERATING BOARD OF SMYTH LTD.).

DAISY SPORT   **DESIGN DIRECTOR 1979–1982**
- INVOLVED IN CHANGE OF COMPANY DIRECTION FROM TRADITIONAL DOUBLE KNITS TO WOVEN COORDINATES.
- FULL RESPONSIBILITY FOR DESIGN OF 5 LINES PER YEAR, DIRECTING A STAFF OF 10.
- RESEARCHED PIECE GOODS MARKET AND DEVELOPED PRINTS, YARN DYES, AND NEW SOLID VEHICLES EXCLUSIVELY FOR COMPANY.
- ESTABLISHED PETITE DIVISION AND SET STANDARDS FOR FIT. FINAL RESPONSIBILITY FOR MISSY & LARGE SIZE DIVISIONS AS WELL.
- CO-DIRECTED ALL NATIONAL SALES MEETINGS AND WORKSHOPS.
- SELECTED OUTFITS AND OVERSAW PHOTO SESSIONS FOR ADVERTISING.

113

DESIGN BACKGROUND

- ROSS LTD. 1976–1979
  JUNIOR BLOUSE COMPANY.
- MISS MANDY 1975–1976
  DESIGNER AND PRINT STYLIST.
- D. S. JRS. 1972–1975
  JUNIOR DIVISION OF DAISY SPORT.
- CHARLES AND CO. 1971–1972
  STARTED THIS CONTEMPORARY COMPANY AS A
  DIVISION OF ROSENAU BROS. DESIGNED FIRST 5
  SEASONS RESULTING IN $4 MILLION VOLUME
  FIRST YEAR.
- DAVID BROOKS 1968–1971
  DESIGNER FOR SWIMWEAR DIVISION.
- ELLEN HOLMES 1967–1968
  CO-DESIGNED LINE.
- PINEAPPLE STREET 1964–1967
  DESIGNER FOR ALL FOUR DIVISIONS INCLUDING
  "BEACHES."

EDUCATION

PRATT INSTITUTE—B.F.A. 1964

PROFESSIONAL AFFILIATIONS

- A.W.E.D.
  American Woman's Economic Development
  Corp.
- FASHION GROUP

EXAMPLE #3: CHRONOLOGICAL RÉSUMÉ

ALICE RICHTER

30 EAST 23rd STREET

New York, New York 10010

Home (212) 555-6477

Office (212) 555-6900

SUMMARY:
- Senior Executive with proven success in management and hands-on creative work in the retail, fashion and beauty industries.
- Strong communicator experienced in all phases of creating and developing effective, exciting images for companies/products.
- Professional capable of shaping and motivating a creative staff to produce the materials needed to achieve a company's business objectives.

CAREER HISTORY: 1984 to Present

COSMETICS LABORATORIES, INC.

Vice President—Creative Services
- Developed sales training approach for retail counter consultants in 1,800 stores emphasizing usefulness of gift-with-purchase items and resulting in increased sales during GWP promotions.
- Successfully expanded acclaimed "silent series" advertising campaign to include seven additional products; selecting products to be featured and coordinating creative production.
- Developed a new art department; hired and trained a complete staff increasing productivity and creativity.
- Initiated in-house graphic art production procedures reducing production costs by 88% per season.
- Initiated search for a new beauty model, increasing product visibility, and upgrading company image.
- Work directly with major New York stores on implementation of advertising themes ensuring appropriate projection of company and product images.

115

1977 to 1983 **STUART FRANK ALLEN**
Creative Director of Advertising
- Responsible for selection, training and supervision of creative staff involved in all aspects of SFA's advertising. During my tenure, improved employee relations/employee satisfaction, eliminating high turnover in department.
- Conceptualized and executed effective advertising campaigns for specific divisions, private label, new store openings.
- Worked directly with designers and manufacturers developing ad campaigns designed to enhance and appropriately project the image of both store and vendors.
- Scripted and supervised production of internal communication videotapes, increasing awareness of systems, procedures and merchandising trends throughout a 41-store network.
- Among the people trained and supervised, two left SFA to become Vice Presidents and Co-Creative Directors at an advertising agency; one to become a Creative Director at an agency; two started successful free-lance businesses on their own; another became Marketing Manager of the Catalog Division.

1962 to 1977 **LR&K ADVERTISING, INC.**
Brand Manager and Creative Director 1975–1977

Copy chief 1971-1975

Assistant Director of Advertising 1962–1971

EDUCATION: BA Communications
Northwestern University 1962

EXAMPLE #4: CHRONOLOGICAL RÉSUMÉ

SUSAN MORROW
12 Custer Lane
Bethesda, MD 20817
Home (301) 555-7320
Work (301) 555-9291

PROFILE

FINANCIAL SERVICES PROFESSIONAL with eight years diversified international banking experience. Innovative vice president with successful track record implementing a breadth of complex assignments requiring strong leadership, problem solving, communication and advanced conceptual and analytical skills.

CAREER HISTORY

FINANCIAL BANK, BETHESDA, MD 1980–Present
Credit Deputy, International Private Banking, 1987–Present
Manage $162 million credit portfolio in Latin America, Asia and Europe. Developed and taught in-house credit training program.

Regional Credit Supervisor, 1986–1987
Responsible for corporate credit approval for North Asia and Europe, with emphasis on Capital Markets products.

Manager, Credit Training Program, 1985–1986
Directed training program for World Banking Group. Responsible for management and evaluation of 120 officer candidates per annum. Monitored content of program for line relevance.

Representative in Thailand, 1984–1985
Managed $120 million portfolio comprised of sovereign risk, trade finance, corporate lending and correspondent banking.

Correspondent Banker, South East Asia, 1980–1984
Extensive travel in Asia, including six-month assignment in Hong Kong Branch as Credit Analyst in 1980. Responsible for 150 accounts.

EDUCATION 1975-1980

COLUMBIA UNIVERSITY GRADUATE SCHOOL OF BUSINESS, New York, N.Y.
M.B.A. Finance and International Business, January 1980.

HUNTER COLLEGE, New York, N.Y.
B.A. Asian Studies and Journalism-summa cum laude, Phi Beta Kappa-June 1978.

SPECIAL INTERESTS
Working knowledge of French, Mandarin, Thai.
Australian Citizen-U.S. permanent resident since 1973.
Extensive travel throughout Australia, New Zealand, United Kingdom, Europe and Asia.

EXAMPLE #5: CHRONOLOGICAL RÉSUMÉ

ELLEN SPECTOR
154 Lombard
SAN FRANCISCO, CA 94111
(415) 555-0033

PROFILE: Multi-talented individual with four years experience in corporate sales, marketing and public relations. A highly organized self-starter with excellent written and oral communication skills.

EMPLOYMENT   TURN KEY OPERATIONS (TKO) November
EXPERIENCE: 1983 to Present

Sales and Marketing Manager, San Francisco
Responsible for sales, marketing, advertising and public relations including:
* Receiving, tracking and closing all sales calls/leads
* Developing advertising schedule and negotiating advertising contracts
* Conducting public relations campaigns to business community, Chamber of Commerce and existing clients
* Writing newspaper articles, making presentations and producing quarterly newsletters
* Creating and implementing new marketing strategies
* Producing collateral materials
* Shopping and evaluating competition
* Negotiating client leases and renewals

March 1988 to October 1988
Assigned to Los Angeles on a project basis to supervise start-up of new HQ Fox Plaza/

119

Century City location. Responsibilities included hiring, training and managing three salespeople.

February 1987 to February 1988
Assigned to New York to supervise start-up of Crown Building/Fifth Avenue location. Took center to $2,400,000.00 in annualized revenue over a 9-month period by achieving 100% occupancy.

Sales Representative
October 1985 to January 1987
Took center from 50% occupancy to 100% occupancy in 6 months. Won TKO National Sales Representative of the Year 1986.

Assistant Operations Manager
February 1985 to October 1985
Promoted from Corporate office to field location. Supervised five telephone operators and managed all telephone service for clients.

Personnel Assistant
November 1983 to January 1985
Maintained files for 500 employees. Scheduled interviews. Administered insurance benefit program.

EDUCATION: University of California, Los Angeles
Bachelor of Arts, History, December 1982

EXAMPLE #6: CHRONOLOGICAL RÉSUMÉ

BARBARA JOFFE
Editor/Writer
22 WEST 68TH STREET
New York, NY 10023
(212) 555-5320 (Home)   (212) 555-1234 (Office)

STAFF POSITIONS

Associate Travel Editor, BRIDE'S Magazine, The Condé Nast Publications, Inc., NYC
'86 to Present
Develop travel story ideas, research and write two to three major by-lined articles and various shorter pieces every issue, assign and edit two to three free-lance features per issue, direct on-location travel shoots.

Assistant Travel Editor, MODERN BRIDE Magazine
Cahners Publishing, NYC
'82–'86
Researched and wrote one to two major by-lined articles and Trip Tips column every issue, fact-checked and proofread galleys, selected and coordinated travel slides.

Corporate Travel Assistant
The Condé Nast Publications, Inc., NYC
'79–'82
Arranged travel (airlines, hotels, car rentals) for all CNP employees.

CONTRIBUTING WRITER

Magazines: Travel & Leisure, Diversion, Caribbean Travel & Life, Vintage, European Life, Teen Traveler,

Books: Penguin and Fodor's guidebooks

121

EDUCATION   Boston University, B.A. Degree in Greek
                   Classics, graduated 1979

                   College Year in Athens Inc., Greece, attended
                   1977–78

OTHER   New York University, "Magazine Editing"
STUDIES: "Intro to Photography"
                   Swedish Institute, Swedish 1-4
                   International Center of Photography,
                   Photo 1-3
                   Columbia University, Word Processing

                   **REFERENCES AND PORTFOLIO
                   ON REQUEST**

EXAMPLE #7: CHRONOLOGICAL RÉSUMÉ

LISA ROSARIO
2 KINGS TERRACE
PARADISE VALLEY, AZ 85253
(602) 555-0000

SUMMARY
Twelve years experience servicing mortgages, developing and implementing sound collection procedures on $3-billion real estate portfolio, and instituting guidelines for maintaining insurance on corporate investment portfolio.

EXPERIENCE

MONTFARE FUNDING
Phoenix, AZ

MORTGAGE SERVICING MANAGER   1988–Present
Responsible for developing mortgage servicing division, instituting effective quality control procedures for HUD and secondary investors (FHLMC and FNMA). Overseeing all mortgage servicing functions from escrow analysis to liquidations.
- Supervise preparation of monthly investor reporting.
- Develop servicing manuals and guidelines for secondary investors and in-house mortgages.
- Develop FNMA & FHLMC monthly investor reports and accounting on Financial Industry Computer Systems (FICS).

TROUT BROTHERS
San Francisco, CA

MORTGAGE COMPLIANCE ADMINISTRATOR   1987–1988
Responsible for maintaining servicer compliance program
for 100+ servicers in the secondary mortgage market.
Intensively traveled to review banks' servicing and collection
practices. Extremely heavy telephone contacts and
correspondence follow-up with mortgage bankers, Savings
and Loan Association, and government agencies on servicing-
related changes.
- Supervised staff on $6-million mortgage portfolio.
- Produced compliance manuals and co-authored
  servicing guidelines for purchaser and seller's
  contracts.
- Used Lotus 123 to produce managerial status report.

LIFE INS CO OF BERKLEY
New York, NY 10019

MORTGAGE LOAN SUPERVISOR   1976–1987
Responsible for coordinating day-to-day operations of
mortgage loan division handling $3-billion real estate
mortgage portfolio. Heavy correspondence with 100+ outside
mortgage servicers, attorneys, property asset managers, and
insurance companies personnel.
- Supervised department consisting of 8 personnel.
- Assisted outside servicers to bring delinquent
  loans current and referred loans to attorney for
  foreclosure.
- Negotiated insurance values on real estate acquisitions.

EDUCATION
- Arizona University, AZ, Economics B.A. 1976.
- College of Insurance, CA, Certificate equivalent 1983.

- In-Service training:
  Introduction to the Securities Industry
  Managing for Productivity
  Human Resources for Supervisors
  Oral Presentation Skills
  Effective Corporate Communications

ORGANIZATIONS
- American Management Association (AMA)
- Mortgage Bankers Association of America (MBA)
- National Association of Insurance Women (NAIW)

EXAMPLE #8: CHRONOLOGICAL RÉSUMÉ

JAYNE BARKLEY
8 CHASE PLACE
CHEVY CHASE, MD 20815
(612) 555-0000

PROFILE: *Seasoned marketing communications executive with extensive experience in strategic marketing, advertising and sales promotion. Primary skills in analyzing, conceptualizing and presentation. Strong organizational, analytical, quantitative and communications abilities.*

ABEX PRODUCTS CORPORATION, CHEVY CHASE, MD
1987-Present
Manufacturer of industrial speciality protective coatings and paint

DIRECTOR OF MARKETING: Established and manage new marketing department for this fast growing, privately owned corporation. Responsibilities include:
- Developing and managing all marketing activities in order to assure company growth and profitability
- Creating and implementing annual marketing plan and budget
- Analyzing and/or forecasting competitive markets and trends
- Planning and implementing all advertising and promotional activities
- Administering and coordinating marketing department budget

HART & MASTERS, BALTIMORE, MD 1985–1987
Manufacturer of products for the custom picture-framing market

ADVERTISING MANAGER: Established and managed advertising department for this new division of a manufacturer of graphic arts materials.
Responsibilities included developing, planning and supervising:
- All advertising, sales promotion and direct marketing programs to support the marketing plan
- Annual budget
- Departmental staff in the execution of advertising and promotional objectives

126

- Packaging design, in-store P.O.S. and fixturing
- Trade show exhibits
- Advertising agency activities
- Creation and implementation of all advertising department systems and procedures
- Supplier resources for maximum cost efficiency

BALTIC COMPANY, BALTIMORE, MD 1984–1985
Manufacturer of underwater sports equipment

SALES PROMOTION MANAGER: Established and managed in-house promotion department.

Responsibilities included:
- Consumer and trade promotions to support marketing plan
- Promotion budgets
- Sales promotion planning, procedures, scheduling and systems
- Annual promotion plans
- Retail co-op programs
- In-store P.O.S., fixturing and packaging design
- Supplier resources

MANGAN CORPORATION, NEW YORK, NY 1978–1983
Manufacturer of textiles for the home furnishings and auto markets

DIRECTOR OF ADVERTISING: Ran in-house advertising agency for seven operating divisions.
Responsibilities included:
- Creating, implementing and administrating advertising programs
- Management of in-house agency
- Supervising media, production, traffic and product publicity departments

EDUCATION

PACE UNIVERSITY, PLEASANTVILLE, NY-B.S., MARKETING 1977
THE WESTERN COLLEGE OF MIAMI OF OHIO UNIVERSITY, OXFORD, OHIO
1973-74

EXAMPLE #9: CHRONOLOGICAL RÉSUMÉ

MARGARET ARCHER
P. O. Box 1
Riverdale, NY 10471-0136
212-555-1111

SUMMARY: Ten years of solid fund-raising experience on behalf of major cultural and educational institutions in New York City; additional experience through voluntary service as a board member for other non-profit organizations.

PROFESSIONAL EXPERIENCE:

Women's College, New York, NY (1988–present)
Director of Major Gifts
- Develop Nucleus Fund Plan in preparation for launching Centennial Campaign;
- Identify, screen and rate top prospects for gifts of $100,000 and above;
- Manage detailed investigations to assess financial capabilities of prospects;
- Plan and organize stewardship events to acknowledge donors of $100,000 or more;
- Brief and debrief President, faculty members, and senior staff members participating in cultivation and solicitation activities;
- Work with capital campaign consultant and other members of senior management team to develop strategies and materials as the campaign takes shape.

Botanical Gardens, Cypress, NJ (1987–88)
Manager of Major Gifts
- Worked with Leadership Gifts Committee to develop solicitation strategies for and to secure major gifts of $100,000 and above to the Garden's Centennial Program;

128

- Prepared and wrote major individual, foundation, and corporate proposals and solicitation materials;
- Briefed and debriefed President and members of the Leadership Gifts Committee on all solicitation activity;
- Served as Development staff liaison with Acting Vice President for Science and Director of the Atrium.

Major University, New York, NY (1984-86)
Associate Director of Development,
Business School
- Managed the Affiliated Business Fellows Program, a group of 100 corporations which provided student financial aid, faculty research funds and general operating support;
- Organized and coordinated the Business School's Annual Dinner in 1985 for more than 1,100 guests at the Waldorf-Astoria; worked with the Alumni Association Board of Directors and its Annual Dinner Committee;
- Secured major, multi-year gift in support of faculty research in the marketing of financial services;
- Directed the Annual Fund Campaign targeted at an alumni base of 24,000 (achieved a 34% increase in 1984–85).

Museum of Art, New York, NY (1981–84)
Associate Development Officer, Grants
- Managed all aspects of foundation and government fund-raising, generating $1 million a year toward general operations and designated programs;
- Implemented the foundation strategy for the "Save the Arts" campaign in 1982, a campaign which raised $1.25 million within a two-week period.

The Museum of Sculpture, New York, NY (1979–81)
Grants Officer
- Raised $1.8 million from state and federal government sources during 1980-81, including major grants to support capital renovation, special projects, and general operations;
- Worked with the Director of Membership and Development on securing corporate grants for special exhibitions.

Associates Advertising, San Francisco, CA (1977–78)
Account Coordinator
- Worked as part of account management team on major client accounts.

EDUCATION: National Endowment for the Arts, Arts Management Fellow, 1977
Women's University, A.B., Dramatic Art-Dance, 1976

EXAMPLE #1: FUNCTIONAL RÉSUMÉ

HELEN MILLER

400 N. WABASH AVE.
CHICAGO, IL 60611
TEL (312) 555-2685

EXPERTISE

Energetic, resourceful Apparel Executive with over fourteen years experience and responsibility in the following areas:

MERCHANDISING
- Planned financial objectives.
- Established and coordinated merchandising themes.
- Targeted deliveries of product to stores through involvement in production scheduling and effective planning to deadlines.
- Merchandised the design of up to four lines simultaneously.
- Negotiated prices of, and bought, piece goods both domestically and off-shore.
- Created and purchased finished garment import and 807 programs.

MARKETING
- Anticipated consumer needs and established a marketing strategy for pricing, promotion, and distribution.
- Created all brand identification material for product packaging and advertising.
- Developed and coordinated company advertising campaign.
- Maintained targeted gross margin objectives.

DESIGNING
- Researched international markets and trade shows.
- Designed moderate and better-priced ladies coordinated sportswear, separates and suits.

131

- Supervised a design and pattern making team with responsibility for fit and quality.
- Developed private label merchandise for retail buyers.

EMPLOYMENT HISTORY

SASSY GIRL, INC.
1985–Present

Vice President Merchandising and Design

Merchandise and design girls 4-14 sportswear line. Diversified product mix increasing volume 25% to over $20 million.

CONCEPTUAL MERCHANDISING, INC.
1983–1985

Owner, Merchandiser and Designer

Founded private label ladies suit and sportswear company with volume of $14 million.

SNAP DRAGON, INC.
1980–1982

Vice President Merchandising and Design

Merchandised and designed private label junior and ladies sportswear lines. Increased volume over 3-year period from $15 to $40 million.

SASSY GIRL, INC.
1973-1980

Design Director

Rose from position as a store shopper to Design Director responsible for divisions with combined volume of $30 million.

EDUCATION

BA, University of Connecticut 1972

EXAMPLE #1: COVER LETTER

320 San Vincente Blvd.
Los Angeles, CA 90048
April 1, 1990

Jane Parsegian
Vice President
The IMB Corp.
1001 Wilshire Blvd.
Los Angeles, CA 90024

Dear Ms. Parsegian:

During a recent phone conversation with a mutual colleague, Andrea Stone, I learned that your company is seeking a new director of personnel. I believe that my ten years of experience with a competitive Fortune 100 company make me an excellent candidate for this position.

As you can see from the enclosed résumé, I have a fast-track record of accomplishments in employee benefits. In my last position, as employee benefits director, I was actively involved in funding, costing, and mergers and acquisitions. I was also solely responsible for creating a highly innovative benefits program for top management, which was eventually adapted for all levels of employees companywide.

I would appreciate an opportunity to discuss my credentials further at your earliest convenience and will be in touch with you shortly to see if we can set up an interview time. In the meantime, please feel free to contact me should you have any questions or require any more information.

Thank you so much for your time and consideration.

Sincerely,
Audrey Cranwell

EXAMPLE #2: COVER LETTER

547 Comstock Avenue
Syracuse, NY 13210
May 20, 1990

Jerry Lichtenberg
Executive Vice President
Andrew R. Freedan, Ltd.
736 Fifth Avenue
New York, NY 10019

Dear Mr. Lichtenberg:

Congratulations on the opening of your newest midtown division! It sounds like a wonderful opportunity for your company and, since you are looking for a new director of corporate leasing, a terrific opportunity for me as well.

I am a strong leasing broker with seven years of professional experience in the field. As you will notice on the enclosed résumé, my perseverance has paid off for my previous company with a host of key accounts, including ABC Cosmetics, Union Club Bank, CBC Hardware Stores, and Uncle Ralph's National Supermarkets. Now I would like to use my proven abilities in negotiating with such a diversity of clients to build your corporate leasing program into a major profit center.

Should you desire any more information, including references, I will be happy to provide whatever you might need. I will contact you shortly to see if we can set up an interview at your earliest convenience. In the meantime, thank you so much for your time and attention.

Sincerely,
Deidre Danson-Cowen

EXAMPLE #3: COVER LETTER

270 Valley Green Drive
Atlanta, GA 30342
July 7, 1990

John Furman
President
Sweets Candy Company
1 Sweets Lane
Atlanta, GA 30307

Dear Mr. Furman:

Ms. Jane Gordon, executive vice president of Tollman Food Corp., suggested that I contact you. She mentioned that your company is expanding overseas and we both felt that my background, interests and expertise match your firm's needs very well.

Over the past fifteen years, I have played a key role in the development and direction of several food companies both in the U.S. and abroad. Most recently, I served as managing director of D&D Gourmet's subsidiary in Japan, where I also initiated and negotiated the purchase of Fuki Foods, a company specializing in low-calorie gourmet products.

I've enclosed my résumé and a few press clippings to give you a more complete picture of my credentials. I would, however, appreciate an interview at your earliest convenience so that we might discuss my background and your needs further. I will be in touch with you soon to set up a mutually convenient meeting date. Thank you so much for your time and consideration.

Sincerely,
Carolyn Smith Tanner

EXAMPLE #4: COVER LETTER

1701 Superior Avenue
Cleveland, OH 44114
August 17, 1990

Janet Haddock
Director of Personnel
Best Advertising
178 Jones St.
Cleveland, OH 44114

Dear Ms. Haddock:

I read with great interest the ad you ran for an account executive in *The Plain Dealer*. As I hope you will see from the enclosed résumé, my four years as a junior account executive for Thomson & Bendit Advertising have given me the kind of experience that will make me an asset to your firm.

Specifically, I worked with several key media accounts at Thomson & Bendit, including *ABC Magazine* and *The Everyday News*, as well as such cosmetics firms as *Beauty Works* and *ZYX Cosmetics*. I myself brought in *The Goods Company* and *America's Beauty Stores*, a 200-store chain headquartered here in Cleveland. In total, I was responsible for nearly $1 million in billing last year alone.

I will call your office within the next few days to see when you might have the time to meet with me. Thank you so much for your time and attention.

Sincerely,
Jennifer Mangan

7.

Networking: Marketing "Me, Inc."

Here's a riddle: What do you and McDonald's have in common? (Well, true, you both have buns. But let's get serious.)

The answer is that you and McDonald's are both companies with something to market and promote. The only difference is that the fast-food chain employs hundreds of experts to market its burgers, fries, and shakes. And all you have is you.

You are your company. You're the chairman, marketing director, public relations officer—even the product. Think of yourself as a firm called "Me, Inc." You've already decided on your advertising campaign goal (objective) in chapter 5 and created your "commercial" résumé in chapter 6. Next, you've got to get out there and sell yourself.

The best sales approach is a blitz marketing campaign called networking. Though much has been written about it, few women (including myself when I lost my job) truly understand what it is or how to put it into practice.

I'm sure you've heard the term "good-old-boy network"—the business fraternity to which all men belong simply by virtue of their gender. This network allows them to connect with and get help from other men for whatever professional needs they have, whether it's scoping out a potential client, checking a new accountant's reference, or finding a new position.

Until very recently, businesswomen have had to cope without such a network, mostly because there were so few women in the management ranks of corporate America. But there are other reasons women haven't been able to help each other effectively. One is that, as little girls, most of us were encouraged to play games like jacks, hopscotch, jump rope, and "house," all independent pastimes that did nothing to foster the team spirit so essential to networking.

Further, says Mary Scott Welch in her book, *Networking: The Great New Way for Women to Get Ahead*: "In a funny kind of way, it [networking] seems unfeminine. . . . The average woman grows up waiting for the phone to ring, waiting to be asked (to dance, to marry), not choosing but waiting to be chosen. Even if she later rejects that lady-in-waiting concept intellectually, she still 'feels funny' about pushing herself forward. She's never crashed a party in her life; the very thought of doing so is repugnant."

The result of all this conditioning is that women often don't feel comfortable asking others for assistance. As Tessa Albert Warschaw, author of *Rich Is Better*, says, many women feel undeserving: "They have trouble asking for and expecting help."

I agree. But I think these discussions ignore a very important point: Women may have trouble asking for help, but they are terrific at eliciting information. Just think: How many times have you said to a friend or even a passing acquaintance, "I love your hair. Where did you get it cut?" or "What great business cards. Who designed them?"

And what you may not have realized when you asked these questions is that you were engaging in a form of networking, because that's largely what networking is—asking for (and hopefully, getting) information. Now all you need to master is how to do it with your professional goals in mind.

At this point, some of you may be asking, "Why do I need to network at all? Can't I just read the want ads, apply for the position, interview, and, if I'm sharp enough, get the job?"

Let me answer with a statistic: Some 80 percent of all jobs are obtained through personal contacts, according to a recent Harvard University study. Approximately 10 percent are obtained through the classified ads and another 10 percent through executive recruiters. And when you consider that good executive recruiters are a lot less likely to present you as a job candidate when you're out of work, the statistics change somewhat, making personal contacts the path to nearly 90 percent of jobs. It's to your advantage, then, to learn all you can about networking.

Know What You Want

Some people try to "network" by going around aimlessly telling everyone they meet their tale of woe and saying, "I need a new job. Is there *anything* in your company?" Then, when this tactic doesn't pay off with a position, they berate themselves for being "unemployable."

But there are good reasons why such an approach doesn't get you anywhere. First, it sends out negative signals to potential contacts. After all, if you think of yourself as a loser and convey that to your listeners, why should they disagree? Second, asking if there's "anything" available at a company doesn't clarify what you want. And last, if you pose the question "Do you know of anything at your company?" or "Can you help me?" you're asking for a yes or no answer and are not allowing your contacts to offer any options in between. By putting them on the spot, you're increasing your chances of getting a no.

Instead, what you need to do to network effectively is to figure out what you want and the best way to ask for it *before* you speak to a single contact.

Hopefully, you've already decided what you want by the time you've reached this chapter. If you haven't, you need to do what I call Stage One networking. First, choose the job fields you want to explore, then ask yourself, "Who would know the kind of person I need to meet?" and write down their names and numbers. Once you've identified these people (that is, those who know the right people), call each one for a referral and make a list of prospective contacts. Now you can begin moving into Stage Two of your networking campaign by calling as many people on that list as possible, in as many areas as you're exploring, and asking them for information about their fields.

Suppose you were considering working for an executive recruiting firm that specializes in the hotel industry. First, you would make a list of anyone you can think of who would know the kind of people you want to meet. For instance, suppose Joanna, an old college friend, is the director of public affairs for a major hotel chain and uses executive recruiters whenever she's short-staffed. Put her on your first list.

Next, contact Joanna and ask her to recommend someone (or, preferable, several people) at the recruiting companies she deals with who might be willing to speak with you. Just say something like, "I'm in the process of researching the hotel recruiting field. I've already read up on it, but I need to know more. Do you know anyone I might speak with?"

Once you get a name, call that person—it's easier than a cold call because you can use your friend's name as your entrée—and explain your goal: to learn more about the hotel recruiting field. Then request half an hour of her (or his) time so that you might ask a few questions. Once you're in her office, you have a great opportunity to gather information with a few well-chosen questions, such as:

- "Since this is such a specialized field, I'm curious about how you got into the industry and why." (Remember, people love to talk about themselves!)
- "What portion of this kind of job is soliciting new accounts and what portion is actually meeting job candidates?"

- "Who would you say are the top companies in this field?"
- "What is the range of compensation one can expect in the first year?"
- "I really appreciate the time you've spent with me. Is there any chance that you could recommend one or two more people I could speak with?"

With just a few questions, look at all you've accomplished. First, you've shown the person that you've done some homework and are serious about the field. (By the way, if you're also researching other fields, don't mention it. As far as this contact is concerned, hers is the only one you're considering.) Second, you've learned a lot about the industry and this particular recruiter, both of which will help you if you ever return looking for a position.

Shifting Your Motive

Once you've done some preliminary networking and decided on the field (or company or position) for you, you need to move into Stage Three networking. Now your motive has shifted slightly; you're not just looking for information, you're also looking for a job.

At this point, the list of possible contacts in your chosen field should be fairly extensive—and ever-growing. (In effective networking, one contact often leads to another and another and another. . . .) But once you know what career you want and you're networking to find a job, the kinds of questions you ask your resources change a bit. Let's use the hotel recruiting field again as an example.

- "How did you get into this field and why?" (Shows that you're interested in the person and respect what he or she has achieved.)
- "Do you know of any companies that are planning as-yet-unannounced expansions in the near future?" (Demonstrates your resourcefulness in seeking new job opportunities.)

- "The trend today seems to be for recruiters to open up their own one- or two-person shops. How is that affecting your company's business? If you were in my position, is going out on your own something you would consider?" (Shows your understanding of industry trends as well as your willingness to be flexible in exploring new options.)
- (For career-changers.) "To the best of your knowledge, will the three major companies in this industry consider a newcomer, or should I target my job search to one of the small firms?" (Reveals that you have some understanding of the complexity of the field.)
- (For career-changers.) "My travel agency background has given me a lot of contacts in the hotel industry. Would it be inappropriate for me to submit a list of them with my résumé?" (Shows that you have good contacts, which may pique the contact's interest in you as a potential employee.)
- "I read the *Wall Street Journal* article on your company last week and was surprised to learn it's only three years old. What triggered that kind of growth?" (Demonstrates that you've done your homework and that you're not just wasting the person's time with idle conversation.)
- "I really appreciate the time you've spent with me. Could you recommend anyone else that you think I should speak with?" (Again, shows your commitment.)

But Does It Work?

These networking appointments often lead to job offers. To understand how, let's play out a few possibilities.

Suppose you know you want to be a hotel executive recruiter and you've networked yourself into an appointment with the senior vice president of one of the best firms. The worst-case scenario is that you'll spend thirty minutes of your meeting with someone who gives you some good information but who doesn't offer to connect you with anyone else and doesn't offer you a job.

But better scenarios are more likely.

- The person you're talking with thinks you're terrific and recommends that you speak with four of his contacts. This will broaden your network and get you more networking appointments, one of which may lead to a job.
- Your networking appointment gives you good information and leads you to a few more contacts. You think that's the end of it, but the very next week his secretary calls you with the number of another hotel executive recruiter who just happened to mention over a lunch date that she's looking to expand her staff. Presto—an interview, and a possible position!
- You're in luck! Two weeks after your networking appointment one of the firm's new recruiters quits suddenly and guess who gets the first interview?
- You go on a networking appointment, and unbeknownst to you, the company needs a new recruiter but has been so involved with an enormous new hotel account, that it's had no time to do a search. When you walk in the door, the timing is perfect and you get the job.
- The interviewer thinks you're terrific. So terrific, in fact, that he decides to put you on staff at his company, creating a new position tailored to your strengths.

What you're actually doing in Stage Three networking is tapping the hidden job market; that is, finding a job that no one else knows is available before it has a chance to be advertised. (In fact, because many companies want to avoid the expense of an executive recruiter, and/or the time it takes to sift through the hundreds of responses to a want ad, they often *rely* on office networking to find good candidates.) It's no wonder that 80 percent or more jobs are gotten this way. Take what happened to Margaret, for instance.

Margaret Archer, a professional fund-raiser, was the director of major gifts for a prestigious women's college. She had been wooed there from another top-notch job, but seven months later she was fired. What to do?

"Well," says Margaret, "I knew I needed to network, and the first person I called was Jack, whom I'd worked for before. I explained my situation, noting that I was now available for new opportunities. He said he'd keep his ears open, but that he didn't know of anything at the moment.

"The very next week, though, he got a call from Phil, someone he knew in fund-raising. Phil informed him that he needed to fill a position at his firm right away. Apparently, he had had a consultant working on a three-month contract and, though there was more work to be done, the consultant had another commitment and could not stay. So Jack called me and told me what Phil had said. The next phone call I made was to Phil to arrange an interview for the following Monday.

"At that appointment, I met with Phil, another person I'd be working with, and the consultant who was leaving. The next morning, the company called me for references, and by Friday I had an offer."

Networking Right

Now that you understand what networking is and how it works, let's take note of a few tips on how to do it right:

(1) NEVER PREJUDGE ANYBODY

Admit it; we all do it. We walk into a party or professional luncheon and size up the room. Too often, we decide whom we want to talk with and whom we want to avoid based on preconceived notions. Well, that's a habit that needs to be broken.

Anne Luther's story illustrates why. As vice president of public relations for Möet Hennessy, Anne had to attend many industry functions. At one particular luncheon, she was seated at one of those large round tables that don't allow you to comfortably chat with anyone except those people on either side of you. Anne turned to the man on her right and after introducing herself, found out that he was an insurance salesman.

With all apologies to any readers who are in insurance, Anne thought to herself "Boring!" and as casually as possible, turned to the man on her left. And guess what? Another insurance salesman. Well, Anne, who's pretty savvy and who was in the process of getting divorced, figured, "If I'm going to have to speak to an insurance salesman, I might as well talk to the cuter one," and swiveled back to try to strike up a conversation with the man on her right.

After a few moments, Anne learned that his specialty was insuring big-name rock and roll groups. A rock and roll freak, Anne said, "Really? Do you ever get to go to any of the concerts?" "Sure," he said. "I live backstage."

Always thinking, Anne asked him if they ever served food and drinks backstage, and when he said yes, she asked if they would consider using her company's product. (Good press for her firm; good deal for the rock groups.) He was more than interested and the two of them decided to meet a week later to continue the discussion.

During the course of their next meeting, he told her about the charity work he'd been doing in England chairing a music therapy organization to help autistic and mentally retarded kids. When he told her he wanted to bring the program to the States but hadn't a clue about how to tap into the social network that finances such charities, Anne told him that not only was she familiar with that network but that Möet would be willing to underwrite the first U.S. event.

One year to the day after their initial meeting, the first charity event was held in the States, starring such names as Phil Collins and George Michael (whom Anne got to meet). Today, that program is helping autistic and mentally retarded kids across the entire country. Not bad for a little lunchtime networking!

(2) DEVELOP A, B, AND C LISTS

Another homework assignment: Get out your professional and personal phone books and use them to compose three lists. First, create an A list, consisting of decision makers; that is, all the people who are in a position to offer you a job. Don't worry if this list is short. You'll soon come up with more names.

Next, devise a B list. This one consists of anyone you know who could network you to people for your A list, such as past suppliers, fellow members of professional organizations, or former colleagues.

Your C list consists of everyone else in your life who might possibly know a B list person, including old college roommates, neighbors, second cousins, your aerobics instructor, and your hairdresser. Don't edit anyone out. You never know who knows someone who knows someone who knows someone.

Once you've constructed your lists, you can start making your phone calls. Begin with the C list. Reason? Calls to these folks offer a no-risk chance to practice asking for information and an opportunity to get comfortable with your "script." It's the same approach stand-up comics use. They try out their acts at small clubs, honing their jokes and tossing out the duds until their routines are polished enough for prime-time TV. You're polishing your presentation for the contacts on your other lists.

When you're ready—say, after a week or so—start calling everyone on your B list. Only graduate to your A list when your new networking skill is well developed and you are completely at ease with your script.

Keep in mind that your A, B, and C lists will keep growing as you continue to network, so don't worry if you never make it through them all. In fact, if you're networking right, you'll never really finish because the number of contacts will always be multiplying.

(3) GET A PERSONAL BUSINESS CARD AND ANSWERING MACHINE

If you followed the WINbreaker tips in chapter 1, you've already taken care of this. But just in case you haven't, let me reiterate that a personal business card will help prevent the worst-case scenario of networking: You meet a wonderful contact and have to fumble around for a place to scribble down your name and number. Not very professional, is it? So get a card inscribed with the pertinent information. And get an answering machine, too; don't sabotage yourself by not having a machine or phone service to take messages in your absence.

(4) LEARN TO ASK FOR SOMETHING BY *NOT* ASKING FOR SOMETHING

A while ago, I said that networking is basically asking for information. Well, that's true, but networking also involves another element that's even more important: connecting yourself with people who have the power to hire you without putting them on the spot.

I used to live in a high-rise apartment where I had what I call "elevator friends." I'm sure you have a few yourself. You know, you can tell when they've been on vacation because you notice that great tan, and you have some idea of what they do for a living because, after all, that's often how we identify ourselves, at least initially.

Now let's say you've lost your job selling ad space because the magazine you worked for folded. But you remember that Barbara, one of your elevator friends, is the sales manager for a local radio station. Since you love ad sales and wouldn't mind changing media, Barbara is a perfect target of opportunity. But you've got to approach her properly. If you use too direct an approach, you'll cut off your opportunities by making it easy for her not to help you.

First, we'll play out what you *shouldn't* do:

SCENE ONE, TAKE ONE (You've lost your job and two days later you find yourself alone in the elevator with Barbara.)

YOU: "Hi, Barbara. We missed you at the tenants' meeting last week."

BARBARA: "Yes, I know. I got stuck out of town."

YOU: "Lucky. We just rehashed the same old business. And speaking of business, I don't know if you heard that my magazine officially folded last week and I'm looking for something new. I was wondering if there were any sales openings at your company?"

BARBARA: "Not that I know of. But if I hear of anything I'll let you know."

End of scene . . . and end of that networking opportunity. You blew it by directly asking for a job and giving Barbara an easy way out. Now let's try a better approach:

SCENE ONE, TAKE TWO

YOU: "Hi, Barbara. We missed you at the tenants' meeting."

BARBARA: "Yes, I got stuck out of town."

YOU: "Lucky. We just rehashed the same old business. And speaking of business, I don't know if you heard, but my magazine officially folded last week and since I was in sales, I'm now exploring using my expertise in other media. Didn't you once tell me that you sell advertising time for radio?"

BARBARA: "Yes, for the last ten years now."

YOU: "That's what I thought. I'd love to find out a bit more about that field. If I were to call you at your office, is there any chance we could set up an appointment so I could find out just what radio sales entails? I know you're busy, but I wouldn't need much time; and I'd really appreciate it."

BARBARA: "Sure, no problem. I'd be glad to help."

YOU: "What's the best time to call?"

BARBARA: "I'm usually in all morning."

YOU: "Great. I'll call you tomorrow when you have your appointment book in front of you so that we can set something up. Thanks so much!"

End of scene, but not end of story. Now you'll have an opportunity not only to gather information but also to sell yourself to someone who may well be in a position to offer you a job or at least help you tap into the hidden job market.

(5) BRUSH UP ON YOUR NETIQUETTE

No, it's not a typo. "Netiquette" is a term Lynne and I invented to combine the terms "networking" and "etiquette" because, truthfully, there are certain rules of decorum you should follow to be an effective networker. That is, it's simply not enough to blankly accept a networking lead by saying "Thank you." If someone has been helpful enough to give you a contact—say a former co-worker has offered you the name of her colleague, Diane—then in addition to expressing your immediate appreciation, you need to know enough netiquette to follow up gracefully. To do this, you might have to ask your initial contact some of the following questions:

- "Since you don't have Diane's number with you, would you like me to call you for it or will you call me?"
- "Can I use your name when I call Diane?"
- "Would you prefer to speak to Diane before I call or should I just go ahead and contact her?"
- "Do you want me to call you to make sure you've had time to mention me to Diane?"
- "What's the best time to reach her?"

It's also possible that someone may know the perfect person for you to talk with but she or he doesn't really know that person well. In that case, when you make your contact, netiquette dictates that you begin the conversation by explaining how you got his or her name and why you are calling. For example, you might say, "I was at a professional luncheon last week where several people mentioned that you specialize in financial planning. I'm really interested in that field, and I was wondering . . ." (Then explain what you want.)

You get the gist. What's important is to make everyone involved feel as comfortable and receptive to your call as possible.

As I write this, I feel more like Emily Post than Emily Koltnow, but I have to say that following up EVERY networking contact with a thank-you is essential. A phone call to your original contact will suffice, although a written note is better. In either case, be sure to thank the person for the referral and let him or her know how the contact went.

Here are a few sample thank-you notes:

Dear Christie:

Thank you for recommending me to Ann Row at Watkins Ltd. I contacted Ann and have set up an appointment to meet with her next Wednesday for breakfast.

I'll let you know how it goes, but in the meantime, thanks again for all your support.

Sincerely,
Julie Whitmeyer

Dear Claudia:

I'm so glad we met at the NAFE luncheon last week. I can't tell you how much I appreciated your setting up an appointment for me with George Heller. I spoke with him yesterday, and he not only agreed to meet with me, he gave me the name of five colleagues to call as well. Now that's networking at its best!

I'll keep you posted as to my progress. But for now, thanks again.

Best regards,
Kathy Dwyer

For the networking people who gave more generously of their time, a slightly more elaborate written note is a must. Here are some more samples:

Sharon Burns
Vice President Sales
Utica In.
555 Fifth St.
Morganville, WA 12345   January 12, 1990

Dear Ms. Burns:

I just wanted to drop a brief note to thank you for the time you spent speaking with me yesterday. The perspective you offered on the printing industry was very informative. I never realized how many new avenues are available to explore.

I've already followed through on one of your suggestions and started reading the book you recommended. I know I have a lot of work ahead of me, but meeting with you has given me a great start.

Thanks again for all your help.

Sincerely,
Greta Mason

Chris Palmer
Marketing Director
The Bowles Company
West Road
Andover, MI 12345   May 16, 1990

Dear Chris:

I can't tell you how appreciative I am that our mutual friend, Alicia Gross, brought us together. I really enjoyed our lunch—the conversation as much as the terrific pasta.

Thanks for setting up the appointment for me with your human resource department. I met with Peter Roberts yesterday and you were right—there is an opening in the corporate communications department that would be perfect for me. I have an interview scheduled for next week. I'll let you know how it goes.

Again, I want to thank you for your encouragement and assistance. Next time, lunch is on me!

Best regards,
Judy Rizzo

Once Is Not Enough

Networking is like brushing your teeth; it's something you should do automatically every day. Whether it's making a couple of phone calls, writing a thank-you note, going to a professional meeting, or even attending a social gathering, you should be out there constantly nurturing your network of contacts. This is especially true when you're out of work, but it's also important even after you resituate yourself. More on that in the last chapter.

You'll be amazed at how quickly your network grows. To monitor your progress, I suggest you keep a networking chart. It's something I did when I lost my job and began meeting so many new people in so many different industries. All you have to do is put a circle with the word "ME" in it in the center of the page. As you meet new people, connect your circle with their names; then, as they introduce you to new contacts, write those names into your chart. You can also include what happened as a result of the contact so you can see who led you to what events. In a sense, you're creating a family tree, only this time you're growing your family of professional contacts.

At the end of this chapter is my chart, at least for the first eighteen months after I was fired. Take a look at it. It reflects how networking helped me start my business, write this book, appear on television, and, best of all, meet lots of wonderful, interesting people.

Remember, networking is a numbers game. And you already know a great number of people. I would estimate that the average adult knows approximately 300, including professional acquaintances, the people you've met in cooking class, at the health club and at other recreational activities, old school mates, professionals (your doctor, lawyer, accountant), neighbors, relatives, and friends. Just think about that the next time you're attending an industry luncheon and there are eight people at your table—you have a potential opportunity to meet 2,400 people from that one afternoon alone! But it's up to you to tap into all the possible resources.

Networking works.

So do it.

Now!

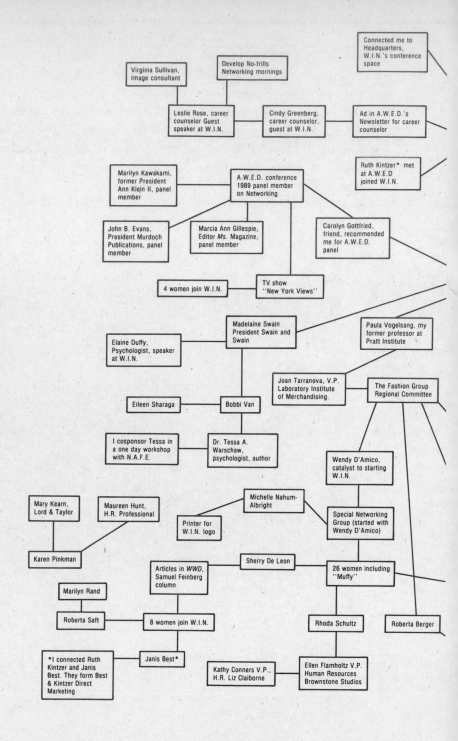

Virginia Sullivan, Image consultant

Develop No-frills Networking mornings

Connected me to Headquarters, W.I.N.'s conference space

Leslie Rose, career counselor Guest speaker at W.I.N.

Cindy Greenberg, career counselor, guest at W.I.N.

Ad in A.W.E.D.'s Newsletter for career counselor

Marilyn Kawakami, former President Ann Klein II, panel member

A.W.E.D. conference 1989 panel member on Networking

Ruth Kintzer* met at A.W.E.D joined W.I.N.

John B. Evans, President Murdoch Publications, panel member

Marcia Ann Gillespie, Editor Ms. Magazine, panel member

Carolyn Gottfried, friend, recommended me for A.W.E.D. panel

4 women join W.I.N.

TV show "New York Views"

Madelaine Swain President Swain and Swain

Paula Vogelsang, my former professor at Pratt Institute

Elaine Duffy, Psychologist, speaker at W.I.N.

Joan Tarranova, V.P. Laboratory Institute of Merchandising.

The Fashion Group Regional Committee

Eileen Sharaga

Bobbi Van

I cosponsor Tessa in a one day workshop with N.A.F.E.

Dr. Tessa A. Warschaw, psychologist, author

Wendy D'Amico, catalyst to starting W.I.N.

Mary Kearn, Lord & Taylor

Maureen Hunt, H.R. Professional

Michelle Nahum-Albright

Printer for W.I.N. logo

Special Networking Group (started with Wendy D'Amico)

Karen Pinkman

Sherry De Leon

26 women including "Muffy"

Articles in WWD, Samuel Feinberg column

Marilyn Rand

Roberta Saft

8 women join W.I.N.

Rhoda Schultz

Roberta Berger

*I connected Ruth Kintzer and Janis Best. They form Best & Kintzer Direct Marketing

Janis Best*

Kathy Conners V.P., H.R. Liz Claiborne

Ellen Flamholtz V.P. Human Resources Brownstone Studios

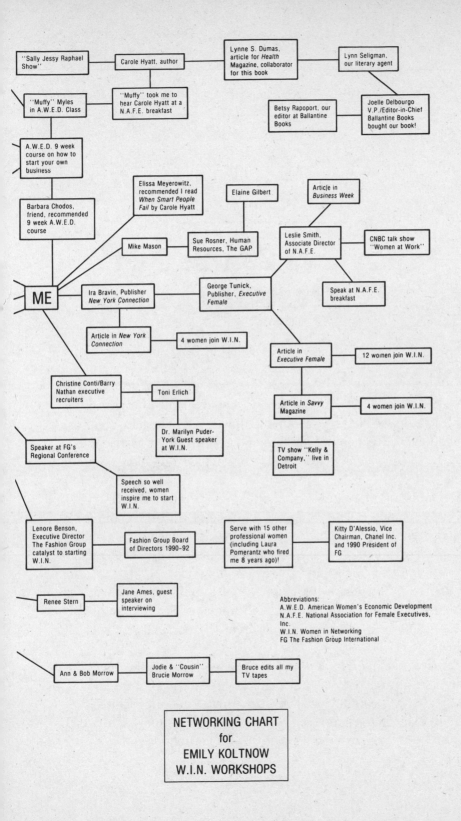

"Sally Jessy Raphael Show"

Carole Hyatt, author

Lynne S. Dumas, article for *Health* Magazine, collaborator for this book

Lynn Seligman, our literary agent

"Muffy" Myles in A.W.E.D. Class

"Muffy" took me to hear Carole Hyatt at a N.A.F.E. breakfast

Betsy Rapoport, our editor at Ballantine Books

Joelle Delbourgo V.P./Editor-in-Chief Ballantine Books bought our book!

A.W.E.D. 9 week course on how to start your own business

Elissa Meyerowitz, recommended I read *When Smart People Fail* by Carole Hyatt

Elaine Gilbert

Article in *Business Week*

Barbara Chodos, friend, recommended 9 week A.W.E.D. course

Mike Mason

Sue Rosner, Human Resources, The GAP

Leslie Smith, Associate Director of N.A.F.E.

CNBC talk show "Women at Work"

ME

Ira Bravin, Publisher *New York Connection*

George Tunick, Publisher, *Executive Female*

Speak at N.A.F.E. breakfast

Article in *New York Connection*

4 women join W.I.N.

Article in *Executive Female*

12 women join W.I.N.

Christine Conti/Barry Nathan executive recruiters

Toni Erlich

Article in *Savvy* Magazine

4 women join W.I.N.

Dr. Marilyn Puder-York Guest speaker at W.I.N.

Speaker at FG's Regional Conference

TV show "Kelly & Company," live in Detroit

Speech so well received, women inspire me to start W.I.N.

Lenore Benson, Executive Director The Fashion Group catalyst to starting W.I.N.

Fashion Group Board of Directors 1990–92

Serve with 15 other professional women (including Laura Pomerantz who fired me 8 years ago)!

Kitty D'Alessio, Vice Chairman, Chanel Inc. and 1990 President of FG

Renee Stern

Jane Ames, guest speaker on interviewing

Abbreviations:
A.W.E.D. American Women's Economic Development
N.A.F.E. National Association for Female Executives, Inc.
W.I.N. Women in Networking
FG The Fashion Group International

Ann & Bob Morrow

Jodie & "Cousin" Brucie Morrow

Bruce edits all my TV tapes

NETWORKING CHART
for
EMILY KOLTNOW
W.I.N. WORKSHOPS

8.

Interviews Can Be Fun
(Trust Me)

If you could spend no more than a few hours dressed up in your favorite power suit telling an attentive company executive how wonderful you are—and then be rewarded with a sum equivalent to your last annual salary or more—would you do it?

Me, too. And that's how you should look at interviewing.

I mean, suppose you go on two interviews with the same firm and spend about three hours of your time, after which you accept a position with a compensation package of $45,000 a year. That comes out to $15,000 per hour—not bad pay, in my book!

I know I'm fudging a little here; you'll actually have to work a year to get the full $45,000. But the point remains: Rarely in our lives does so small an investment of time hold the possibility of such a big payoff.

Think about interviewing as your chance to be in the spotlight rather than on the hot seat. After all, you're not going into enemy territory. On the contrary, you've been invited to someone's office after he or she has either seen your résumé (you know, the great one you wrote after reading chapter 6) or heard about you from an executive recruiter or mutual acquaintance. So you are both welcome and qualified.

Consider this, too: You are also needed.

Most likely, you're being interviewed for any of three typical reasons. First, the firm needs to fill an existing slot left open by someone who quit. Second, the company is not happy with an individual employee and is looking to replace him or her. Third, the firm is starting a new division or expanding its current staff and is creating a new position for someone with your talents. So in addition to being invited and qualified, you are also in demand.

What's more, interviewing can be fun. (See, I told you to trust me.) It's a bona fide opportunity to be a legitimate busybody. You can visit other companies—often, your former competitors—get a peek at their offices, and possibly meet the people you've either read or heard about through various industry channels.

Another fun part of interviewing lies in its similarity to show biz. You're the star, the actress playing the part of the confident, perfect candidate. It's your job to engage the audience (i.e., the interviewer) with your award-winning (make that job-winning) performance. And you don't even have to worry about stage fright; at the end of this chapter, I'll run through an exercise that will pump you up for your debut by putting you in a positive, assertive frame of mind.

One more plus about interviewing: You begin with a clean slate. You're innocent of all the company's politics—and it's innocent of yours. For the moment, all the prospective company knows about you are your past accomplishments and the way you handle yourself in the interview, so you're off to a fresh start.

Before You Say Hello: Interview Preparation

In my past, I was very naive about interviewing. Each time I began a job hunt, I assumed that my solid professional reputation, sense of humor, attractive appearance, and ability to put people at ease would make all potential employers naturally receptive to hiring me and job offers would just pour in. I was wrong.

Although I knew that the interview was important—experts say that 95 percent of employers hire on the basis of a personal interview—I didn't realize that there was something I could and should have done before the interview to increase my chances of being offered a job. And that is research.

Yes, research. Again. But before you start groaning, consider this good news: Because you're out of work, you have the time to research properly. In fact, you have the edge over those poor working souls who have to squeeze any interview prep time in between appointments, if they have time to prepare at all.

Basically, there are two ways to research right:

(1) THE OBVIOUS

Call people you know and see if you can connect with anyone who works, or has worked, for or with the company with whom you will be interviewing. Try to find out who's really in charge, the personalities of the key executives (especially the person you'll be interviewing with and/or reporting to), the "personality" of the company itself (supportive, competitive, fast-paced, laid-back), salaries, dress code, firing history, how the firm is perceived within the industry, and company growth potential. Also see if you can discover why the spot you're interviewing for is vacant. If it's not vacant, try to learn who is currently in that position and why he or she is being let go.

(2) THE NOT-SO-OBVIOUS

Get thee to a library. If you're interviewing with a public company, find a copy of the annual report. If it's not in your local business library, just call the company direct; it will be glad to send you one. Then read the report, especially the first section, to learn about the firm's financial status, officers, and general direction.

Also, bone up on individuals within the company, the firm itself, and the industry in which it operates by reading any recent newspaper or magazine articles in both the trade and consumer press. While you're sorting through publications, pay attention to any advertising the company might have run. The ads will reveal to you how the firm wants to be perceived.

Finally, if the company deals in goods rather than a service, go to a store and see what the product line looks like. Then spend some time thinking about how it measures up to its competition.

What you want your research to yield is the who, what, when, why, and how of the company and its industry. Your goal is to be able to converse knowledgeably, even to the point of using industry buzz words, during the interview.

It's important to give yourself as much time as possible to research effectively. Even if you have only a day's advance notice, do what you can; finding just one person who's familiar with the company or reading a single article could give you a valuable leg up on the other candidates.

Whenever Jane Ames, president of New York–based Interfocus, a company that teaches interviewing techniques, guest lectures at WIN Workshops, I insist that she tell one personal story that clearly illustrates the benefits of proper interview research.

Jane was called to interview for a vice presidency overseeing the shoe division of a major mass merchandising retail chain. But the only experience with shoes in Jane's past was shopping for her own— not exactly the glowing credential she'd need to win a spot at this national firm. So Jane, who was then "between situations," did some quick and intensive research.

She started at the library, but hit a dead end when she discovered that *Footwear News*, the most influential trade publication of that industry, was not referenced. Since she knew it was published in New York, however, she called the publishing firm and asked if she could go up to the offices and look at back issues. After obtaining permission, Jane spent the better part of one day reading, taking note of buzz words and key industry issues and trends.

Once she felt she had a fix on the shoe business at large, she made a field trip to the nearest company store and scrutinized the shoe department. She even "borrowed" a couple of hang tags (those labels that hang off products), which she felt she could use in her interview.

Well-armed with information and presentation material, Jane had a terrific interview. She felt confident and relaxed, was able to answer questions intelligently and even ask a few of her own. The result? A job offer, and one she firmly believes would never have come her way had she not researched so thoroughly.

More Prep Work

In your entire career, how many interviews have you had? Ten, twenty, fifty . . . a hundred? Ever wonder why nearly every interviewer asked you many of the same exact questions?

The reason is that interviews are usually conducted by managers, vice presidents, or even presidents of the company, most of whom have had no training in how to interview. As a result, they turn to the same few books, which list the same interview questions, such as "What are your weaknesses?" and "Where would you like to be in five years?"

Even though such repetition can be tiresome, it works to your advantage because it gives you a chance to prepare many of your answers in advance. In fact, the last section of this chapter includes the twenty questions you most likely will be asked during an interview—and suggested answers to the five toughest ones you'll hear if you've been fired. Read them carefully and begin preparing your own responses.

While you're at it, remember to be precise. Women, usually more verbal than men, have a tendency to go on too long in answering interview questions. Try to fight against longwindedness by practicing a one-minute, thirty-second, and fifteen- or even five-second response to the same question. But keep in mind that, like a good actress, you want to sound as spontaneous as possible, so don't memorize every word of your answer; instead, become comfortable with the message you want to convey and a few key phrases that will best get it across.

WIN TIP: To give your response a fresh take when you've been asked one of those if-I-get-asked-this-one-more-time-I'll-scream questions, enthusiastically say something like "Oh, that's an interesting question. Let me think a minute." Then pause before delivering your already-prepared answer. If you do it right, not only will this give the impression that your answer is totally unrehearsed, but it will also make the "typical" interviewer feel good for asking a thought-provoking question. (See, interviewing *is* acting.)

Dress the Part

Thank God, we've passed the days when dressing appropriately for an interview meant wearing a navy or gray suit with a complementary silk tie. And perhaps *you've* passed the point where you feel you need some advice about what to wear on an interview. But a few do's and don'ts are still worth mentioning:

• Never wear perfume. Even though it may be your signature fragrance, the person who's interviewing you may hate it—or worse, be allergic to it. So why take the risk?

• Dress appropriately for the particular corporate culture. Obviously, the financial community will be more staid than the advertising industry, but even within finance, some companies will have a more relaxed corporate image than others. If possible, visit the offices before the interview and scope out what everyone's wearing.

• Dress for the particular position for which you're interviewing. If you are interviewing with an art supplies manufacturer to head its in-house advertising and public relations, you should probably dress with more creative flair than you would if you were interviewing to be its vice president of finance.

Jane Ames points out another aspect of dressing suitably (no pun intended): Know how to manipulate your image to your advantage. Jane has dark olive skin, an angular face, and straight black hair, so when she interviews for a high-powered position, she emphasizes these naturally strong features. She pulls her hair straight back and wears a vividly colored jacket and large, angular jewelry, all of which adds up to a visually powerful and assertive image. In the past, though, when she was interviewing for lower- and middle-management positions, she'd wear soft colors and change her hairstyle so that it fell loosely around her face, thus conveying a more gentle and less aggressive message.

ANOTHER HINT: Once you choose an interview outfit, put it on and sit down in front of a mirror. Make sure that the skirt isn't riding up too high, that the jacket keeps its shape, and that, most of all, you feel comfortable.

Getting There—On Time!

Murphy's law comes into play whenever you go out on an interview, so prepare yourself for a flat tire, traffic jam, unavailability of cabs or public transportation, or anything else that could prevent you from being punctual. Give yourself PLENTY of time to spare.

If you live in a rural or suburban area and you're heading into unfamiliar territory, stake out the route and location of the building the day before so that you know exactly where you're going. Make sure you also check out parkway exits and detours; the last thing you want to do is add to your anxiety by getting lost. In a major city, always know the cross streets as well as the street address, so you'll have your bearings.

The point of all this effort is to arrive as much as half an hour before your appointment so that you have the time to prep yourself properly. It will allow you to get a cup of coffee or just sit in your car and do the following.

(1) Reread your résumé to remind yourself of all your accomplishments and any points you want to get across during the interview.
(2) Go over the answers you've rehearsed so that they're fresh in your mind.

(3) Do some deep breathing to relax.

(4) Pump yourself up.

Let me elaborate on this last tactic. At each WIN Workshop group, I put the women through an exercise that helps psych them up for an interview. I begin by asking all the women to close their eyes, but since this is not a practical maneuver while you're trying to read a book, keep your eyes open and read on.

GETTING-PSYCHED EXERCISE

You're going to go on three imaginary interviews. The first two, with Company A and Company B, have been arranged by an executive recruiter. In each case you've been fired from your last job and are now looking for work. (Something I think you can understand—all too well!)

Interview #1

Your appointment at Company A is at 10:00 A.M. and you arrive on time. It's located in a part of town you hate, the building is horrible, the elevator is so decrepit you're almost afraid to step inside. The office itself is no better, cluttered with dusty plastic flowers and a hodgepodge of mismatched furniture. Loud rock music blares from the radio of a receptionist whose gold-painted fingernails are long enough to earn her a place in Ripley's Believe It or Not.

You're kept waiting thirty minutes, during which time you ask yourself about a hundred times, "What am I *doing* here? They'd have to *double* my last salary to get me to work here." Then, Mr. Abbot, the company president, enters. He's exactly what you had envisioned, smelly cigar butt and all. Without apologizing for the delay, he leads you into his messy office, the centerpiece of which is a musty moosehead mounted on the wall, and starts his questioning.

Now, think about how you would feel during this interview. Are you on your toes or inattentive? Impatient or relaxed? Are you giving enough thought to your answers?

If you're like most people, you probably wouldn't give your best interview because you wrote the company off even before you began. You would race through your answers, not bother to ask any of the questions you prepared, and in general do whatever you could to bring the meeting to a fast finish.

Interview #2

Now, imagine you're at Company B. Out of your entire industry, this is one of the few firms for which you'd really like to work. To top it off, it's in your favorite part of town, you love the building, there's a little coffee shop in the lobby, and you already see yourself stopping there every morning to pick up a blueberry muffin. As you enter the office, you're overwhelmingly impressed. Fresh flowers bloom everywhere, the decor is lovely, soft music plays in the background. After the receptionist takes your name, he apologizes and tells you that Mr. Berkley is running a little behind schedule and will be with you in ten to fifteen minutes. Then he offers you a sparkling water and you settle in to wait with a copy of the company's latest annual report. You think to yourself, "I want this job more than anything! I'd even take a substantial cut from my last salary to work here."

Precisely ten minutes later, Mr. Berkley comes out to greet you and you're charmed on sight. He reminds you of your favorite uncle, Ralph.

Now, pause again. How do you feel as you walk into his impeccable but comfortable office? Is your anxiety building or are you calm? Do you remember everything you rehearsed or has your mind gone blank? Are you talking too fast or too slow?

Chances are, this interview would have gone better than the one with Company A, but you still probably would not do your best because you felt you had too much riding on it to be relaxed and in control. As a result, you might ramble on for too long with your answers, not ask your questions, and even forget to bring up that important article on the company you read in *Forbes* last week. By the time you return home, your shins will be black and blue from kicking yourself.

Interview #3

You now have a high-paying job you love, a super office, and a wonderful staff. One day, another executive recruiter calls and says that the president of Company C would like to meet with you. Company C happens to be one of the best companies in your industry and you are flattered. You go on the interview. But remember; now you're gainfully and happily employed.

How do you feel during this meeting? Are you more confident than you were when you went on the other two interviews? Do you feel you're in a better or worse negotiating position?

It's my guess that you would feel most comfortable and secure on interview number three. You already had a job that you liked and for which you were well compensated. Your ego was stroked because a good company was trying to steal you away, and your confidence was at an all-time high. Thus, you gave your best interview for Company C.

The lesson of this exercise is simple: To pump yourself up before any interview, try to re-create the situation surrounding Company C in your mind. Even when it's not true, tell yourself that you're currently working at a job you love, that you're well paid, and that this company would be lucky to have you. That way you'll greatly increase your chances of turning in your best interview performance.

You should do this exercise even when you're interviewing with your version of yukky Company A. Know why? First, to practice. The more interviews you go on, the better you get.

Second, to go for the offer. You want to get as many job offers as possible, even one from Company A. Because when you're interviewing with other companies, it's wonderful to create the impression that you're in demand by being able to tell them that you have another offer—they don't need to know from whom.

Third, to keep the door open for future contacts. Even when turning down a job from Company A, do it with grace. Thank the interviewer very much for his offer and tell him the only reason you are not accepting at this time is that the position doesn't offer "something" you want, and then make sure it's "something" his company can't possibly offer, such as international travel, a chance to learn sales, whatever. You might also offer to recommend other candidates, through the recruiter, who you feel would be suitable. After all, you never know who Mr. Abbot knows—maybe even the president of Company B, or C—or D, E, or F. And who's to say he wouldn't recommend you to them, particularly since your dealings with him have been so gracious?

The Interview Emergency Kit

An interview is too important to let some small annoyance or mishap keep you from looking and doing your best. Suppose you get something in your eye just before your interview and as you tear up, your mascara starts running. And speaking of running, there's the typical panty hose predicament. So you can already guess the first two things in the emergency kit you should always take along on any interview—makeup and an extra pair of panty hose.

But there's lots more. Here's a list interview expert Jane Ames and I developed:

(1) Makeup for retouching.

(2) Change of panty hose.

(3) Nail polish for chip touch-ups.

(4) Breath freshener (spray is best; you don't want to get caught crunching on a candy mint when you meet the interviewer).

(5) Reading material in case you have to wait. To make a more professional impression, bring along a trade paper or business magazine and leave Danielle Steele at home. If you're too nervous to read, leaf through your appointment book. Your objective is to look busy and to convey the message that you're always using your time well.

(6) An extra pair of earrings, especially if you wear clip-ons.

(7) Tissues (among other uses, they're good for drying off sweaty palms before an interview).

(8) A purse-size sewing kit for last-minute hem or loose-button repairs.

(9) Safety pins.

(10) Miscellaneous—an extra pair of contact lenses, prescription eyeglasses, or whatever you need to feel secure. One woman in a WIN Workshop told me she takes an extra pair of pumps because she once missed an interview when the heel of her shoe came off.

In addition to those items on your emergency list, always keep a pen and notepad handy, and most important, at least *three* copies of your résumé. You may be meeting with more than one person, and each of them may want your résumé, or the interviewer may ask for an extra copy to pass along to someone else.

Also, bring that typed list of references we talked about in chapter 6. That list should include each reference's title, professional affiliation, and phone number.

Additionally, it's a good idea to bring along the two or three questions you plan to ask the interviewer. Interviewing is a very stressful situation and under the pressure of the moment you might forget to ask something important.

One more tip, courtesy of Jane Ames: If you have a coat with you, always ask the receptionist if there is a place to hang it up. If there is, do so. Not only does this give you one less object to maneuver when you get up to shake hands, but it also sends a subliminal message that you already belong "in" the company, that you're not just an "outsider" waiting for a visit.

The Waiting Game

Good for you. You've done your research and you're well-prepared—well, almost. Before you even get to meet the interviewer, you may have to deal with one more snag: being kept waiting.

Some experts say that if you really want the job, you should wait as long as necessary. But I disagree. I believe that in today's hectic business environment, forty-five minutes is the most you should wait, providing there are no extenuating circumstances. If the interviewer's secretary comes out and explains that the boss is tied up in an emergency conference call and apologizes for the delay, then of course you should stay, provided you won't be late for another *important* appointment. But if you're left waiting without a single explanation or apology and you can feel your anger or anxiety rising, particularly if you have another meeting to get to, then feel free to leave.

Don't do it in a huff, though. Instead, say something like this to the receptionist: "Please tell Ms. Howard that I had another appointment and had to leave, but that I'll call as soon as possible to reschedule the interview." Then leave a copy of your résumé so that you know they have your name and number.

If the interview was set up by a recruiter, I would call him or her and explain what transpired. Then ask to arrange another interview if you and the recruiter feel it's worth it.

The First Impression

Everything you've heard about first impressions is true—they really are critically important. According to Caryl Rae Krannich, author of *Interview for Success*, if the interviewer gets a negative impression in the first five minutes, ninety percent of the time you will not be hired. On the other hand, if you make a positive first impression, you'll get the job a good seventy-five percent of the time.

Jim Brady, director of human resources for Avon Products, confirms this idea. He says: "Regardless of whether it's conscious or not, I do get a first impression. I would hope I work hard enough to understand the whole person, but I think that if the first impression is not positive, then you have an uphill battle. If it's good, then you have the 'halo' effect."

Let me elaborate on Jim's point. When you make a poor first impression, the interviewer's antennae go up and he or she looks for things, quite unconsciously, to reinforce that initial point of view. If you pause before giving some of your answers, the interviewer could construe this as indecisiveness or slow thinking.

To your advantage, if the interviewer's initial take on you is positive, then he or she will be trying, again unconsciously, to confirm his or her first judgment. Thanks to that halo effect, now those pauses will be seen as thoughtful breaks.

That first impression begins as you rise to shake hands, so as trivial as it may seem now, plan on getting up gracefully. Make sure that your handbag and briefcase or appointment book are so positioned that you won't be fumbling as you get up, which could be perceived as unorganized. (Your coat will already be hung up, remember?) In most instances, the interviewer will extend a hand first, but if not, by all means initiate the handshake yourself.

Since your handshake says a lot about you, I'd like to offer a few pointers on shaking hands correctly:

- Stand up straight and make direct eye contact.
- Don't stand too close to the interviewer, or so far away that you have to lunge awkwardly to reach him or her.
- S-M-I-L-E; it helps to register a warm and friendly demeanor.
- Shake hands enthusiastically. Go for the middle ground here; don't crush the person's fingers, and at all costs, avoid a wimpy, lifeless touch. Also, don't pump the interviewer's arm. Just reach out and grasp firmly. (If you can, try to match the other person's web—the space between the thumb and forefinger—with yours. This little trick stops a bone-crushing, and usually male, handshake from causing tears of pain to spring to your eyes and permanently imbedding any ring you might be wearing into the adjacent finger.)
- As you shake hands, introduce yourself—unless the interviewer calls you by name first. Say something like "Hello, Ms. Hammond. I'm Joan Dodd. So nice to meet you." Don't assume that just because she's come out to greet you she remembers your name. She may have interviewed four other people that morning, and will appreciate your refreshing her memory.
- Always address the interviewer formally, using Mr. or Ms. (or Miss or Mrs. if that's how the interviewer refers to herself).

I know all this detail about shaking hands sounds silly, but I'm here to tell you that in every WIN Workshop, only three or four of the women shake hands properly. Some women have a wishy-washy handshake and others feel they have to overcome their femininity by shaking hands like a fullback. So take my advice and practice your handshake with a friend before you begin interviewing.

Inside the Office

Often, after the interviewer ushers you into the office, he or she will ask if you'd like something to drink. I suggest you politely decline. First, you may be nervous and that could show in your trembling hand as you raise the coffee cup. (Let's not even talk about spilling it over your suit or the interviewer's desk.) Second, you'll leave your lipstick on the cup instead of your lips. The only exception to my no-drink rule is if your mouth is parched and you really need to sip something.

Once you're inside the office, use the first minute or so to break the ice by making a comment on something you notice, such as an interesting photo, an award, the view. If nothing catches your eye, talk about the weather, how friendly the receptionist was, the traffic— whatever you can think of to set a pleasant tone and give you (and the interviewer) time to relax and settle down. Of course, if the interviewer initiates the chitchat, which is likely, by all means go along with it.

Now, let me mention a few words about "friendly" body language. Don't sit bolt upright, with your arms tightly folded across your chest. Instead, keep your hands in your lap or resting on the arms of the chair and every so often lean slightly toward the interviewer. Try to appear relaxed, and of course, maintain good eye contact.

Additionally, pay attention to the interviewer's voice; note the pace and tone and try to match it. I'm not suggesting you do a Rich Little–style impression here, but if the interviewer speaks slowly and you're usually at 45 rpm, try to slow yourself down. If you tend to speak loudly and the interviewer is soft-spoken, consciously try to lower your volume. Don't worry if you can't sustain it, but at least try to start off somewhat in sync.

The Twenty Most
Often Asked Questions

I've come up with a list of twenty questions that you'll most likely be asked during your interviews. I recommend writing out the answers to each until you're comfortable with your responses. Keep your responses short and to the point, and always showcase your strengths. Review your answers before each interview, but understand that you'll probably have to modify a few to fit the particular situation. Ready to begin?

(1) Tell me about yourself.

(2) What are your strengths/weaknesses?

(3) Where do you want to be in five years?

(4) Why should I hire you?

(5) What salary are you looking for?/What were you earning in your last position?

(6) Why did you leave your last job?

(7) Why have you been out of work so long?

(8) What do you do in your spare time?

(9) What are your short- and long-term goals?

(10) What aspects of your last job did you enjoy the most/least?

(11) What were some of the problems you encountered on your last job and how did you handle them?

(12) Why do you want to join our company?

(13) Describe your management style.

(14) Why do you think you're the best person for this job?

(15) What kind of boss do you prefer?

(16) Who is the best person you ever worked for and why?

(17) Are you open to traveling and/or relocation?

(18) What were your responsibilities and duties?

(19) If we called your last employer, what would he or she say about you?

(20) Do you have any questions for me?

Sticky Questions for Firees

As I said before, the above are the typical questions you'll usually have to answer during an interview. But if you've been fired, rest assured you'll definitely be asked at least three of them. So let me tackle those and a few other sticky questions now:

Why did you leave your last job?
This query might also be phrased more bluntly as "Why do you feel you were fired?" I can't really suggest an effective response here because the answer will depend on the individual circumstances surrounding your dismissal. But I do suggest that you never say anything negative about your former boss or company in your reply. *Never.*

Even if you feel that your firing was completely unjust, this is not the time to display your emotions. Instead, say something like, "Ms. Winters and I had different styles. She works best adhering to very clear-cut guidelines, whereas I prefer to take a more flexible approach, assessing all the options and choosing the most appropriate for whatever problem. But I'm glad I worked for her because she taught me [or I learned]————" (you fill in the blank).

You and I know that you're really saying "Ms. Winters was a pain in the neck and I'm not." In fact, your interviewer will probably read it that way, too, but he or she will appreciate your tactful style.

Note something else about this script: Not only didn't you say anything bad about Ms. Winters, but you said something positive about yourself and your ex-employer and that will earn you points and head off any more probing questions about your past situation.

WIN TIP: In order to keep yourself in check, make believe that the person you are interviewing with is your former boss's best friend and that the minute the interview is over he or she may pick up the phone, call your ex-boss, and say, "Guess who I just interviewed?" Then answer all your questions accordingly.

Another possible approach is to reply, "The company is taking a new direction and my expertise [and explain what your expertise is] no longer fits the firm's needs." This plays up your strengths and, again, wins you points.

If you've been involved in a restructuring or downsizing, or if your company simply went belly up, then your answer can be more straightforward. Again, though, use the opportunity to emphasize your contributions to your past firm.

Why have you been out of work so long?
Being out of work less than three months is not "long." As I mentioned in an earlier chapter, it takes on average about one month for every $10,000 you were earning to situate yourself again. So if you've only been out of work for, say, two months, don't be intimidated by this question. Simply reply, "It's interesting that you should think that two months is a long time. I used to think that, too, but I've been doing a lot of reading about this recently and I've learned that in today's economy, it takes about one month to every ten thousand dollars you were earning to situate yourself again. But my intention is to beat this statistic."

If, however, you've been out of work for many months, even up to a year, you'll need to come up with a more creative response, such as, "When I first began my job search, I decided that at this point in my career I would only accept a position if it offered me the kinds of career opportunities I most wanted, such as a chance to be involved in a start-up situation where I could have a voice in the company's direction. [Fill in your own goals, but try to tailor them to something you feel this company offers.] Thus far, none of the offers I've had has filled the bill, and that's why I was so interested in your company and meeting with you."

If the reasons you've been out of work so long is that you're making a career change, the question "How come you've been out of work so long?" will be easier to answer. In this case, you'll want to say something like, "This has been a most exciting period in my career because I decided to redirect all my efforts toward making a career change. But doing it right is also very time-consuming. These past several months I've been researching the industry and meeting with many wonderful professionals who have been very helpful. I've had several interviews but to date, no offers that I felt were right for me. And that's why I'm so interested in your company and have looked forward to our meeting."

What salary are you looking for? Or, What were you making at your last job?
Whichever way it's phrased, the real question is, "How much money do you want?" What I find interesting is that most books on interviewing advise you to throw the issue back to the interviewer by saying something like, "That depends on what the job entails" and thus trying to get him or her to name a specific figure.

Well, I think that response is unrealistic.

Like it or not, you are playing ball on their court, and it's up to you to say what kind of compensation you want. Remember that you want to appear open and flexible. The idea is not to lock yourself into any specific figure. You can respond by saying something like "I'm looking for something in the sixties, but I'm open, because at this point in my career finding the right position with the right company is my top priority."

All too often, women worry that they're going to over- or under-price themselves. The only way you'll know for sure what the job pays is if an executive recruiter has sent you. Beyond that, you can only use your professional expertise or your contacts within the company to get a sense of the salary involved. So when you give that ballpark figure, make sure you would be happy accepting it. Be as honest as you can with yourself.

Sometimes during a salary discussion, you will be asked what you were earning on your last job. If you were in a position in which you had a salary and perks (e.g., a guaranteed bonus or stock options), give a ballpark figure for your entire "compensation package," that is, your salary plus perks. Then offer to break it down. Don't lie about your base salary—after all, the interviewer can check it out—but don't sell yourself short, either. Just be "creative" when calculating your perks.

After my last job, I went on a few interviews in which I was asked what I had been earning. I answered, "That depends on today's stock market. My base salary was X, but I had a lot of stock options as well as other perks, which brought my total package up considerably."

If you were on straight salary and had no perks, you should still be honest. Keep in mind that more and more companies will ask to see your W-2 forms or call your former employer for salary verification. (Your ex-boss doesn't have to give the information, but he or she doesn't have to withhold it, either.)

But remember, your honesty won't necessarily hurt you, even if you're going for a sizable salary increase. If you bring important resources, skills, and contacts to the new position, you're a valuable commodity no matter what you were earning previously. I had a client who helped her company franchise its shops. She was so successful that a Japanese conglomerate bought the firm. Within two months she, along with others in the management team, was out of work. Still, she was able to market her franchising expertise to another firm that was willing to pay her nearly twice as much as she had been earning.

There's lots more to say about salary and how to negotiate for your best one, and I'll cover it all in chapter 9. (Be sure to read that chapter *before* you go out on any interviews.)

What are your strengths and weaknesses?
You may not get asked about *both* strengths and weaknesses, but be prepared just in case. First, let's discuss strengths.

This question offers an ideal chance for you to discuss your strongest skills, but you should tailor your response to the specific position. For instance, if you're interviewing for a sales job, stress your cold-calling skills, the fact that you initiated, organized, and ran regional sales meetings for your last company, and/or that you were responsible for the firm's biggest accounts this past year. Your answers should be brief and professionally oriented and clearly demonstrate that you are the best candidate for the job.

Weaknesses are trickier to discuss. I used to use humor to take the sting out of it. When anyone asked me, "What are your weaknesses?" I would pause as if I'd never heard this question before and reply, "Chocolate and Tom Selleck." Hopefully, I would get a laugh, and if the interviewer didn't even crack a smile, I made a mental note that this was not a person I wanted to be working for.

Eventually, though, the question demands a more serious answer. Here again, all the interviewing books tell you to name a weakness that could be interpreted as a strength—for example, "I'm a workaholic." Since I believe that every experienced interviewer has heard that answer before, I suggest you come up with a new twist—honesty.

Think of something that really is a weakness but that won't hurt your chances of getting this particular job. Then name that weakness and explain how you've either overcome or corrected it. As a former vice president of apparel merchandising, I used to say, "I'm not good with numbers, but thank heaven my calculator is."

Or let's say you get so excited about a new project that you want everything done yesterday. You can reveal that, adding, "So I've developed a system whereby I map out all the pieces of the project on a calendar. Then I can look forward to completing each part rather than needing to go from zero to one hundred overnight."

Tell me about yourself.
In interviewing language, this request is called an "open question" because, without directing you in any way, it forces you to make some revealing statements about yourself. But beware: You can sink or swim with your answer.

To reply wisely, bear in mind two important rules: one, keep your answer short, no more than three minutes in length; and two, keep it business-oriented and as targeted to the particular position as possible.

Also, don't lead off with "Where would you like me to start?" and PLEASE don't begin with where you were born. Even though the interviewer is sitting there with your résumé, don't assume that he or she has read it thoroughly—or recently, for that matter. So use this opportunity to highlight your professional accomplishments.

If you were interviewing for the producer's spot on a network TV show, you might say, "For the first half of my career, I worked in front of the camera as a local weathergirl, interviewer, and newscaster. It was really exciting and I learned a lot. But I feel I came into my own when I stepped behind the camera as an assistant producer for KWIN. Even though my title was assistant producer, Alex, my producer, was involved in so many other projects that I was often left to my own devices. As a matter of fact, I actually wound up producing nearly half the shows. And every one of them was done under budget. Last year I was hired as the producer of my own local cooking show, for which I won my first Emmy. And now I feel I'm ready to make the move into network."

I timed this entire response and it took less than a minute. Which goes to show you just how much you're able to say in a very short time if your prepare properly.

Do you have any questions for me?
Your answer to this one should always be a resounding yes. There are two types of questions that you should ask: one geared to give information; the other, to get it.

Questions that give information depend on all that preinterview research I told you to do and will make you stand out from all the other candidates. While they'll be asking ordinary queries such as "What are the benefits?" and "How many weeks vacation do I get?" you'll be asking questions that demonstrate your knowledge of the company and/or the industry. Ideally, your questions should have something to do with the area in which you'll be working. For example, if you're interviewing for a job as vice-president of operations, you could ask, "How much time is the company saving since the introduction of its new computerized shipping system?"

If, however, your research has not yielded anything in your particular line, ask any question that illustrates your knowledge of the company or issues affecting it.

Remember Jane Ames, who interviewed with (and won a job offer from) a shoe retailing firm? After doing her research and discovering a hot industry issue, she was able to ask the interviewer, "What is your company doing about the branded shoe problem?" Clearly impressed, the interviewer answered in detail, which gave

Jane even more information about the firm. Then she whipped out those hang tags she had "borrowed" and said, "You know, I was looking at these and comparing them to your competitors'. And I feel there are a few things that you could do to make your tags more effective." Then she proceeded to explain. Any wonder why she got the job offer?

The second type of question is intended to elicit information not yet discussed in the interview but important for you to know. Such questions might include, "I understand the parent company is moving to the Midwest. How will that affect this division?" or "What is the annual operating budget for this department?" Remember to prepare, and preferably jot down, at least three or four questions before you go in for each interview.

I don't recommend initiating questions about benefits, hours, or compensation until you are actually offered a position, or at least know you're fairly close. Eliciting such information is both premature and presumptuous, and may put you and the interviewer in an uncomfortable spot. Joan Bowman, executive director of staffing and development for Estée Lauder, says that she never brings up any discussion of compensation while conducting initial interviews unless she already has "a pretty good idea that the candidate will be offered the job. Otherwise, discussing salary and benefits gives a false message that you're more interested in the applicant than you may be at that point."

Your Rights to Wrong Questions

Title VII of the Civil Rights Act of 1964 made it illegal for interviewers to ask certain questions, specifically those that request information about your race, gender, religion, or national origins. As a woman, you're probably more likely than a man to be asked illegal questions, mostly because interviewers want to find out what your marital and family commitments are or will be. That's why you need to be both aware of these illegal questions and prepared to handle them.

Here follow some legally suspect questions women are commonly asked. Note that many are not that blatant; instead, they probe for information in a more indirect manner.

- Are you married, engaged, or divorced?
- How long have you been married?
- Are you living with someone?
- Do you have any children and/or do you plan to have any?
- What does your spouse think about your career/traveling/working late?
- Who takes care of your children while you're at work?

You have three choices in fielding these questions. One is to forgo your civil rights and answer. Take care, though; your answers may cost you the job offer. Right or wrong, most employers don't want to hire a woman with five kids, or one who is going through a divorce, or one whose husband's preferences concerning her traveling schedule might impinge on company business.

The second choice is to answer without answering. Suppose you have two kids and you're asked "Who takes care of your children while you're at work?" You might respond with "I don't mean to appear curt, but let me assure you that I never let my personal commitments affect my professional life. I always give 100 percent to my job and nothing less."

You have a third choice if your indignation at having been asked such a personal question outweighs your desire for the position. In that case, you might firmly respond, "I'm sorry, but I consider that question an invasion of my privacy and I will not answer it." Understand, however, that this kind of response will probably put you out of the running.

Occasionally, you'll find a misguided interviewer who asks a legally "iffy" question just to see how you react under stress. Then you may want to opt for the second choice. But how do you know whether the question is a stress gauge or an honest probe?

You don't. So my advice is to answer the first illegal question indirectly; give the interviewer the benefit of the doubt. If any more arise, it's your call.

179

A Final Note

After each interview, send a note thanking the interviewer for his or her time and attention. Be sure to mention the position for which you've applied and briefly restate your special qualifications for the job.

As a sample, here's an effective note I once received:

April 11, 1986

Dear Ms. Koltnow:

It was a pleasure to meet you and discuss current opportunities at Smith & Jones.

The position of Head Designer, as you presented it, would be a good opportunity for me to use my balance of creative, managerial, and technical skills. In addition, your company presents an atmosphere of professionalism that is very appealing.

I look forward to our next meeting, and the opportunity to further discuss these matters of mutual interest.

Thank you so much for your time and attention.

Sincerely,

Ann Gardner

WIN TIP: If your interview has gone well, and you feel the company is interested enough to do a reference check, call your references and prepare them. Just explain that you're up for a particular position and that so-and-so from such-and-such company might be calling them. Then ask them to mention whatever strengths you feel would be valued by the interviewing firm. Try to be as specific as possible, and be sure to vary your suggestions so that the interviewer won't get the same response from three of four different sources.

Before we leave interviewing, let me stress one more crucial point. When interviewing for a job, *particularly when you're unem-*

ployed, your tendency will be to interview with blinders on. Your overpowering need for this job, which stems not only from your financial but also from your emotional state—desperately wanting to be needed again—can blind you to the negatives of the job or company. During the interview you're concentrating on selling yourself, but what you also need to do is size up the company.

Pay attention to such details as how long you were kept waiting, how comfortable you felt, the ambiance of the offices, the attitude and manner of the interviewer(s), and the message they conveyed. Then take some quiet time and ask yourself: *Is this a company that I would like to work for and are these the people I would like to work with?* Try to answer as honestly as you can. Only then will you know not just whether the company wants you, but whether you want the company.

If you decide that this job isn't right for you, then say so graciously and move on. Don't spend time worrying about whether or not you did the right thing; instead, use your energies to prepare for the next interview opportunity. But if you decide to accept the position, then get ready. One of the toughest parts of any job hunt—negotiating your new compensation package—is about to begin.

9.

Negotiating Into Your New Job; Going for the WIN/Win

When we surveyed recently fired women and asked what they would most want in a new position, "fulfilling work," "intelligent co-workers," and "rapport with superiors" ranked high on their lists. While these factors are important, they are certainly no more so than getting a satisfactory compensation package. Yet in our survey, compensation too often took a second, third, or even lower place.

Why? Howard Williams, president of Howard Williams Associates, an outplacement consulting company, believes that "women tend to look at a job in personal terms, e.g., job satisfaction, working environment, co-worker acceptance. They do not view their jobs as men do; that is, in terms of power and authority, which could translate to a better compensation level. Since the value of a job to many women is personal, not economical, it impairs their ability to discuss compensation."

But I think there's something else: the "M" word again. As I explained in a previous chapter, since many women feel a sense of undeservingness, they are uneasy talking about money, much less asking for it. Which is another reason they frequently get less than they could in their job negotiations.

To make matters worse, people who are out of work feel powerless. Since they are not being wooed away from another firm, they feel they've lost their bargaining clout. Thus, as a recently fired woman, you've got lots of extra baggage that needs to be shed before going in to close the deal.

When I speak to women's groups around the country, I often begin by saying that while I was in corporate America, I wanted to come back "in my next life" as an actress. Not for the stardom, not for the chance to be in the spotlight, not even for the money. My reason was that actresses have agents. And agents go in and negotiate your deals.

I wanted my agent to come to me after I got a job offer and say, "Okay, this is what your salary is, these are your perks, here is everything in writing. You start Monday morning." That way, I wouldn't have to haggle about money or go through the awkward, difficult process of fighting for myself.

Who would ever have thought back then that I would one day have a literary agent who would represent me for this book? But I've learned something I never knew before: Although my agent did remove much of the negotiating burden, I was still very much involved in the whole process. And that is how it should be. After all, the result of business negotiations affects you directly. The lesson, then, is clear: Whether you're negotiating alone or with a representative (even one who has your best interests at heart), yours is the name on the dotted line.

Also consider this: The way you handle yourself in your salary negotiations will influence the way you are treated throughout your employ and may very well be the basis for your advancement (or lack thereof) in the organization. That's because all jobs, and particularly executive level positions, require some amount of daily negotiation. Every day you'll negotiate with your staff, suppliers, and colleagues to bring the best out of them. If you can handle yourself well during a negotiation, therefore, you will be viewed as a more valuable potential employee. You will have gained the company's respect.

Gaining respect does not mean being a good little girl and accepting whatever is offered you. Nor does it mean being so pushy and demanding that you alienate your hopefully soon-to-be-new employer. It means calmly, rationally, and objectively negotiating the very best package possible—that is, a deal that's appealing to both parties.

Another factor comes into play here, too. So often when people are out of work, they're ready to accept less money than they're used to making without stopping to calculate how long it will take them to meet, much less surpass, their old salary. But resist this impulse. Remember, your starting salary will serve as a springboard for all future raises and bonuses.

Negotiating makes most of us uncomfortable. But since it's critically important, as well as unavoidable, let's learn how to do it right.

What to Ask For

Set up a sheet of paper to look like this:

I. In Lieu of Salary
   (Example: guaranteed bonus)

   Sales
   (Example: commission)

II. Costs the Company Something
   (Example: early raise review)

   Travel
   (Example: business/first-class)
   Relocation
   (Example: trips back home)

III. Doesn't Cost the Company
   Anything
   (Example: title, if extra perks
   do not come with it)

Now, under the appropriate heading, fill in ANYTHING you could negotiate for. Don't worry about whether it's reasonable for your particular job level or individual industry; this is an exercise to make you aware of all the possibilties.

For example, under "In Lieu of Salary," list anything that you could negotiate for as part of your base salary, such as a guaranteed bonus (an amount of money you will be paid, no matter what, after an agreed-upon period of time). If you're in sales, then under the "Sales" column you might put a commission on top of a base salary.

Under "Costs the Company Something," write down any perk you might want over and above your salary and that costs the company something, such as an early raise review. For those of you whose work involves travel, you might list flying first-class or business-class under the "Travel" heading. Under "Relocation," you might want to negotiate for X number of trips home for holidays and family emergencies.

Finally, under "Doesn't Cost the Company Anything," list any perk that you would benefit from but that doesn't cost the company any out-of-pocket dollars. A title is a good example.

Take whatever time you need to fill in the list as best you can. Then read on to see how many of the following examples you came up with on your own.

IN LIEU OF SALARY

Guaranteed Bonus
Let's say you are shooting for a $50,000 base package, but the company cannot meet that figure because the other four managers at your level are all earning in the low forties. If you were brought on at $50,000 and these managers found out, it could create a sticky political problem. In that case, you might accept a $42,000 base salary—if the firm would agree to an $8,000 guaranteed bonus at year's end.

Sign-on Bonus
Although you don't usually request this directly, the company might offer you up-front money, known as a sign-on bonus, as an incentive to join the firm.

Cash Bonus Based on Profitability
In a privately held company, executives can get a cash bonus when the firm has had a profitable year. This perk is linked not to individual productivity, but to company performance as a whole.

Performance Bonus
If you meet certain agreed-upon goals, your company could give you a bonus, generally based on a percentage of your salary. Typically, such bonuses range from 20 to 100% of your base and are tied in to such performance criteria as sales increases or gains in staff productivity.

Stock
You could be given shares of company stock, which may be a good deal if the company is highly valued and the economy is strong.

Equity in Company
If you're interviewing with a start-up firm that can't afford to meet your salary request, ask for equity in the firm. If the business takes off, you could be in great shape. There is a risk, however, if the company founders.

IN LIEU OF SALARY, IF YOU'RE IN SALES

Commission
Each firm works differently, with commission percentages ranging from one-half percent of your sales on up. Sometimes you'll get a guaranteed base salary plus commission, or even a salary plus commission plus bonus. There are lots of permutations here, so do your

homework and find out what's typical of your industry. Then decide what you want.

(NOTE: Make sure you understand—and get in writing—how your commission is being calculated. Is it on sales booked or shipped? And how do returns, markdowns, co-op advertising costs, etc. affect these figures?)

Percentage of Sales Increase

A company may offer an incentive bonus or percentage of sales on whatever you bring in over and above a certain point. For instance, a company doing $2 million in annual sales might be willing to give you a bonus of $20,000 above commission if you can bring the firm up to $2.5 million within one year.

Account List

Since a salesperson's income often is dictated by the strength of her account list, you should make a strong list part of your negotiation package.

COSTS THE COMPANY SOMETHING

Early Raise Review

If your initial salary has been negotiated down, then it's in your best interest to ask to have your first salary review in three or six months instead of waiting a full twelve months. You might even ask for a guaranteed minimum percentage of increase. I'll tell you why. Carol simply asked for an early review and got one; however, the company said that it didn't see fit to accompany that review with a raise! So learn from her experience.

Also, if the company's policy is to give raises once a year—say, in January—and you join the firm in September, the firm probably won't give you an increase that January (only four months from your start date), but will assume it can wait until the following January— a full sixteen months away. In this situation, I recommend asking for a review date in half that time, or eight months from your start date.

Severance Agreement

A severance agreement is a contract that states that if the company terminates your employment you will be paid a predetermined amount of severance. When I negotiated into my last four jobs, I started each one with a three-month severance agreement.

In one instance, this worked in my favor because the job only lasted four months, yet the firm still had to abide by our agreement. Two weeks later, I landed another job and got the same agreement. This time, however, it might have worked against me because, although the job lasted almost five years, I still only got three months' severance (I might have received more if I hadn't had the contract, but I guess I'll never know.) If I had it to do over again, I would negotiate for three months for the first three years, with one month for each year (or any part of a year) thereafter.

Interestingly, when I discuss severance agreements in a WIN Workshop, everybody always gets uneasy. They don't feel comfortable asking for a "negative" perk. But what's the alternative? You can't ask for a severance agreement *after* you've been fired although, of course, you can ask for severance. To protect yourself, you have no choice but to ask for one going in.

And don't feel that being unemployed at the time of your negotiations works against you. I got three out of my four severance agreements under those circumstances. And if you think I'm alone, just listen to another executive's story.

Betsy was out of work for five months before being offered a terrific position at a political consulting firm. "The offer was wonderful—good salary and excellent benefits, including a great dental plan, comprehensive medical coverage, 100 percent tuition reimbursement, a generous 401K match. But I knew from having researched the company and my department beforehand that I would be walking into a political minefield. I would be working for a very difficult supervisor and I felt there was a chance that the job would not last.

"So, after going through WIN Workshops, I went in and asked for a two-month severance agreement, which is *not* common in my field. The boss said that he would have to take it up with the board; within one week, I had a written severance contract in front of me."

Not only did having that agreement make Betsy feel a lot more comfortable about accepting this job, but the company president, who had negotiated the job terms with her, informed her: "There is now a cost attached to your supervisor not trying to make things work out. I will make it clear to him that your severance will come out of his operating budget." More than one year later, Betsy is still at the job and happily reports that "the politics have now smoothed out and things are going very well."

Health/Life Insurance
Most companies today offer some form of health insurance benefits to their employees, but plans vary widely as to how much you pay and how much the company pays. So you might be able to negotiate for a better package. The same holds true for life insurance.

I must point out, however, that recent government regulations are making it more difficult for companies to offer some of these perks. (See "A Special Note on Section 89," later in this chapter.) But, as I said before, it doesn't hurt to ask.

What you also can ask for is what I call "instant medical." Normally, there's a 90-day waiting period before you are put on the company's group insurance plan. But you can ask that that period be waived and that you become eligible immediately.

Term Contract
A term contract is an agreement between you and your employer that states that you are employed by the company in a particular position for a specified term. It lists your start date, title, salary, area of responsibility, agreed-upon perks, and may include other stipulations, for example, that you may not work for a competing firm for the length of the contract and maybe for some time after, or that you may not hire away staff if and when you leave.

Term contracts work in your favor in that the company cannot fire you unless it pays off the balance of the contract. So if you have a two-year term contract giving you $50,000 your first year and $55,000 the second and you're let go after 12 months, the company must pay you the full $55,000. Of course, the contract will usually

189

stipulate that if you do something illegal, such as stealing from the firm, you can be fired without receiving any compensation.

One of the negatives of a term contract, however, is that after your contract expires you can be let go. So put a clause in to protect yourself. For example, a two-year contract should state that after 18 months of employment the contract must be renegotiated for another term. If the company chooses not to renew your contract at the 18-month point, you've got what amounts to six months' severance while you scout for a new position. Since this is a legally binding document, I strongly advise you to have a lawyer look it over before you sign on the dotted line.

Business Expense Credit Card

If your position requires you to spend out-of-pocket monies to entertain clients, travel, or do research, then you could ask for a credit card that's billed directly to the company. Some companies prefer to offer a cash advance against future expenses. But when I was in corporate, I preferred the former because when I received cash advances, I found I was constantly juggling monies and felt more like an accountant than a merchandiser.

Another word of advice: Don't operate in the red. It is not your responsibility to carry your company in between advances or reimbursement checks, the way Marni did. She traveled abroad so often and spent so much of her own cash that on the day she was fired her company owed her close to $50,000. Almost two years and two lawyers later, she has yet to see that money!

Stock Options

A public company can give you options to buy its stock at the price at which that stock is selling on the day the options are given to you. Then you are allowed to exercise that option, or buy the stock, at that price after a certain amount of time has passed.

For instance, I was once given the option for 600 shares of company stock at $40 a share. I was allowed to buy 200 shares each year over the course of three years. I did that, and when I left the company I chose to sell my shares at $57 per share, making a nice profit.

Support Staff

Historically, the position you're taking on may not come with a secretary or other support staff. If you feel you can't do your job proficiently without an assistant (or assistants), now's the time to bring it up.

Office

Don't assume that you'll have your own office, even if you had one at your former job. If a private office is necessary for your work or position, put it on your negotiating list.

Child Care

A few rare companies have on-site child-care facilities, but if yours doesn't you could negotiate for help in meeting day-care expenses.

Seminars/Workshops

Your company might pay for one-shot classes or seminars that will help you strengthen your business skills, but only if you ask for it.

Continuing Education

It's not unusual for you to need or want an advanced degree, and often companies will either pay the tuition or match your portion of the educational fees. Be aware, however, that there may be a few restrictions. Typically, the courses must pertain to your field, you may be required to get a minimum grade to qualify for reimbursement, or you may have to work for the company for a minimum length of time to be eligible.

Announcement to Clients, Suppliers

Where appropriate, request a printed announcement of your new affiliation and make sure it's sent to past clients and suppliers. This is good press for you and your new firm.

Professional Affiliations
We all belong, or at least should belong, to professional groups, and you may be able to get the company to pick up the annual dues and/ or fees for important association functions.

Car/Expenses
When you need a car to conduct your business and/or have no other way to get to the office, then discuss a company car or car allowance. Don't forget to include such accompanying expenses as parking, gas, maintenance, insurance, and, where applicable, the latest perk—a cellular phone.

Home Office Equipment/Maintenance
If you anticipate having to do some work out of your home, you could ask the company to supply you with a computer, fax machine, copy machine, or whatever else you need to perform effectively. Don't forget to request that the firm pay for maintenance and all accompanying supplies.

Matching Funds for Education
Top-level executives may be able to get the company to match educational funds for their children's schooling.

Executive Dining Room
In some industries and at certain corporate levels, use of the executive dining room is a badge of prestige (important not so much to stroke your ego but to give you more credibility and stature within the firm's hierarchy), as well as an important meeting and networking place. So if you feel it's appropriate, negotiate for use of the executive dining room.

Publications
It's important for you to stay abreast of industry issues, so another perk would be for the company to pick up the tab for pertinent publications. A few that come to mind are *The Wall Street Journal*,

Forbes, and *Business Week*, but don't forget to include titles tailored to your specific field.

Taxi/Car Service
If you know you're going to have to work late, or run around town to lots of appointments, then negotiate for the use of a car or taxi service.

Meals in Office
If you sense that you'll be eating lots of meals at your desk, then you could request that the company reimburse you for them. Some companies even have charge accounts at local eateries to make it easier for their key employees to grab a bite at the office.

Corporation-Held Loans
Some firms, especially larger ones, offer key employees low-interest loans that could be used for a child's college tuition or a down payment on a home. Find out if the company you're interviewing with offers such loans and, if you feel it's appropriate, try to add this to your compensation package.

Financial Planning Assistance
Large companies may be able to offer you free personal financial planning or counseling, which could be a valuable perk.

Health Club Membership
In today's health-conscious society, membership in a health club or cardiovascular fitness program has become a popular perk. You get the feel-good benefit; the company gets a healthier, more productive employee, and, in some cases, maybe even a lower insurance rate.

Prestige Perks
If you're in upper, upper management, you can request such prestige perks as use of the corporate jet, private limo, corporate yacht, company apartment—you get the idea.

TRAVEL

There is a section under "Costs the Company Something" for those of you who are required to do a good deal of work-related travel. Among the benefits you might want to discuss are:

First-Class/Business-Class Travel

If you're going to be making lots of long trips, then being able to go first-class, or at least business-class, is important. This doesn't just hold true for air travel; getting a higher grade hotel or hotel room and an upgraded level of car rental are also valuable.

Don't let "company policy" deter you; several women I know negotiated for and got first-class travel even though it wasn't the norm at their respective firms.

Own Room

You may feel strongly about having your own room when you travel. And even if company policy dictates otherwise, you have every right to ask for it. It's a good idea to present your case based on business priorities; that is, you need to make business calls, want quiet time to catch up on paperwork, or like to get up before dawn to go over your presentations.

Travel Clubs

If you will be using one or two airlines frequently, you could ask the company to pay for membership in airline clubs (for example, Clipper Class, Ambassador Club, and so on). These clubs allow you a place to relax at the airport, make phone calls, or get some paperwork done while waiting for your flight.

Travel Insurance

Not everybody believes in travel insurance, but I do. If you agree, then you can buy an annual insurance policy and ask the company to pick up the tab.

Luggage
Replacing worn or damaged luggage can really set you back, so you may want to ask the firm to reimburse you for new luggage on an as-needed basis.

Telephone Charge Card
When you're on the road, the telephone booth often becomes your office, and a charge card that's billed directly to the company will make things a lot easier.

Calls Home
I call this my E.T. tip. If you're traveling, you should be permitted to keep in touch with your family (within reason, of course) at the company's expense. Don't assume that this will be offered unless you ask for it. I know of one woman whose company restricted her to one call home per week. And if you think that's bad, an unmarried woman in one of my groups worked for a company that would only pay for phone calls to one's spouse. It refused to reimburse her for calls to her mother or fiancé. (I don't make these up, folks!)

Accumulated Mileage
Here, again, companies often have clearly defined policies; some allow you to keep airline bonus miles and others expect you to turn them in to the firm. But since the wear and tear is yours, you may want to ask to retain those miles for your own use. Faye, for example, not only negotiated first-class travel in a company whose policy was "coach-class" all the way, but got to keep any accumulated miles for her own personal use. How did she do it? By letting the company know how important it was to her.

Car Service to and from Airport
The least stressful way to begin and end a business trip is to have a car waiting to take you and your luggage wherever you need to go. Many companies already subscribe to car services and will readily agree to this perk.

195

Car and Driver

When you're traveling to an unknown area in which you have several appointments, it's both stressful and a waste of time to drive around looking for Maple Street. As most of you well know, it also can lead to late or missed appointments and lost sales. That's why asking for a car and a driver may be smart for you and cost-effective for your firm.

Hardship Money

A per-diem allowance of X number of dollars to spend as you wish while you're on the road is sometimes offered by companies as compensation for the stress of travel. Amounts vary greatly, but the figures I usually hear run about $100 to $200 per day.

Comp Time

If you have to travel a lot of weekends, or if you take extensive trips, you can ask for a specified amount of time off as compensation.

Spouse Travel

This is a perk that can be handled in a variety of ways; the company may pick up all travel expenses for an accompanying spouse or may only pay for a portion of the costs. (For example, the company pays for hotels and food, you pick up the airfare.) Children may also be included in this negotiation.

RELOCATION

Salary Adjustment

Let's say you're moving from Ipswich, Iowa, to Atlanta, Georgia, where the cost of living is appreciably higher. Make sure to factor that into your negotiations and ask for your salary to be adjusted accordingly.

Relocation Back Home

I know I mentioned this in the chapter on negotiating out of your job, but it's equally important in negotiating into a new company, so I want to bring it up again. Suppose you are working in a major city such as Atlanta (where you were born and raised) and now you're being wooed away by a wonderful company in Ipswich, Iowa. It's an exciting opportunity, and one you're considering. But while you're at it, consider this: If the job doesn't work out, you'll be far away from home and your contacts there. And since there may well be no other job openings in your field in Ipswich, you might want to return home, where the career opportunities are greater. But if you're in Ipswich and job-hunting in Atlanta, you're competing against other candidates who are already living in your hometown; why would a company want to incur the extra expense of relocating you when there are so many home-based candidates to choose from?

The answer is that it probably wouldn't. And if you have to pay for your return yourself, be prepared to ante up thousands of dollars—moving is expensive. To avoid this messy situation, take some precautions now and make relocation part of your incoming written agreement.

Assistance in Selling/Buying Your Home

Relocating may often mean having to sell your home, which, depending on the current economic climate, may not be easy. Be sure, then, to ask for help. This could mean that the company will buy your home from you and sell it itself, or that it will offer you assistance in paying the upkeep on your home (mortgage, maintenance) until it is sold. The same holds true in buying a new home; the firm could assist you in securing a mortgage, making reasonably priced properties available to employees, and/or picking up closing costs.

Maintenance on Former Residence

Sometimes, it's necessary for you to relocate before the rest of the family can join you, e.g., your kids need to finish out the school year or your husband wants to give two months notice before he leaves his company. You can ask your new employer to assist you in paying the mortgage and/or rent on your old residence until you and your family can settle into one location.

Flatbedding Your Car
If you're making a major move, say from the West to the East Coast, why not save the wear and tear on your car by having your company pay to flatbed your car to your new location?

Storage
Relocation often means you'll have to store some of your belongings until you get settled. Since storage costs can mount up, it's not unreasonable to have the company pay for it.

Trips Home
As I mentioned earlier, if you're relocating, you should consider negotiating for a certain number of trips home during the year for holidays or family emergencies.

Hotel Accommodations
If you're planning to accept the job and finding permanent housing is going to take some time, then the company will put you up at a hotel. But you can negotiate to get the kind of accommodations that will make you most comfortable.

Spouse Repositioning
More and more men today actually relocate for their wives' careers. If that's true for you, you could ask the company to help your husband resituate himself. This could include connecting him with local recruiters, networking him to the business people in town, or perhaps even finding an opening for him in the organization.

Children's Education
You want to make sure that the quality of your children's education remains as high in your new location as it is in your current one.

Therefore, you could ask the new firm for assistance in enrolling your children in the school(s) of your choice.

Language Classes

Relocating overseas may require language classes for you and your family. Why not ask the company to pay for them?

(NOTE: Recent changes in the tax laws could affect your tax liability concerning certain relocation items. So check with your accountant or tax advisor before finalizing your relocation package.)

DOESN'T COST THE COMPANY ANYTHING

Title

Most often, titles come cheap, but they can mean a lot to you and to your career; what's more, they always look great on a résumé. But be aware that in some companies, certain titles come with automatic and expensive perks, such as a private office, a personal secretary, extra vacation time, a higher class of travel, or an expense account. In those instances, be creative and invent an impressive-sounding title that won't cost the company. For example, if you can't be a vice president, then you could ask to be a "senior director" of whatever.

Announcement to the Press

A press release announcing your arrival at the new firm is good publicity for the company and extremely valuable to you. Executive recruiters scour the pages of the business press to see who's where. When they see your announcement, they'll put you into their files— and who knows where that will lead in the future?

Flex Time

Flex time can mean working a different "shift," such as four ten-hour days a week rather than the traditional five eight-hour days. Or it can mean working at a schedule that suits you, whether that's coming in and then leaving early, or perhaps working part of the time at home. But, particularly if you're a working mother, flex time can be an important perk.

Vacation Time

Whether extra vacation time costs the company something or not is up for debate. I believe that it doesn't, because your annual compensation has already been worked out and if you're a professional, you'll make sure your work gets done even when you're not in the office. But others feel that because you're not physically there, the work may be neglected and that does cost the firm something. Whichever category you listed this under, extra vacation time is a good perk to request.

If you haven't had a vacation in a long time (just because you've been out of work doesn't mean you've been on vacation), and the company's policy doesn't allow you to take one for a year, you might want to request a week or so off a little early—say, after six months. If you sense that such a request may generate some static, or if you feel that you need some "mental health" time right away, see if you can postpone your start date and treat yourself to a week off. Also, if you've already scheduled a vacation in advance (for example, a relative's wedding or family reunion) for a period before which you're eligible for time off, make sure to inform your new employer. If you don't get the go-ahead to take the planned vacation with pay, perhaps you can negotiate an unpaid leave of absence for that time.

"Cafeteria" Plans

Many companies now offer a menu of benefits to their employees and allow them to choose which ones they want. For example, if you're already covered on your spouse's medical plan, you may be able to trade your health insurance program for child care or health club membership.

For more ideas, see the following page for a master list with items participants in my WIN Workshops have negotiated for:

Master Negotiating List

I. IN LIEU OF SALARY
Guaranteed Bonus
Sign-on Bonus
Cash Bonus (Profitability)
Performance Bonus
Stock
Equity in Company

SALES

Commission
Percentage of Sales Increase
Account List

II. COSTS THE COMPANY SOMETHING
Early Raise Review
Severance Agreement
Term Contract
Health/Life Insurance
Business Expense Credit Card
Stock Options
Support Staff
Office
Child Care
Seminars/Workshops
Continuing Education
Public Announcement
Professional Affiliations
Car/Expenses
Home Office Equipment/
    Maintenance
Matching Education Funds
Executive Dining Room
Publications
Taxi/Car Service
Meals in Office
Corporation-Held Loans
Financial Planning Assist.
Health Club Membership
Prestige Perks

TRAVEL

First-Class/Business-Class
Own Room
Travel Clubs
Insurance
Luggage
Telephone Charge Card
Calls Home
Accumulated Mileage
Car Service to/from Airports
Car and Driver
Hardship Money
Comp Time
Spouse Travel

RELOCATION

Salary Adjustment
Relocation Back Home
Home Selling/Buying Help
Maintenance on Former Residence
Flatbedding Your Car
Storage
Trips Home
Hotel Accommodations
Spouse Repositioning
Children's Education
Language Classes

III. DOESN'T COST THE COMPANY ANYTHING
Title
Announcement to Press
Flex Time
Vacation Time
Cafeteria Plan (Perk Trade-ins)

A Special Note on Section 89

Before I tell you how to use this list of perks to negotiate the best deal for yourself, I want to emphasize one major point: a government regulation called Section 89 of the Internal Revenue Code. As of now, the law is still being debated and all its whys and wherefores are not yet clearly defined. But the gist of it is to ensure that qualified employee benefit plans do not favor high-paid workers (and, accordingly, do not discriminate against lower-paid ones).

What this means to you is that it may be difficult to negotiate for some of the perks you want. For instance, before Section 89, companies could offer their top execs complete medical coverage even though they did not do so for other staffers; now, they cannot. Also, certain benefits that were tax-free before Section 89 may now be taxable. So check with a human resource professional, accountant, or lawyer to make sure you understand the ramifications of all you're requesting.

How to Ask For Perks

How many of the perks explained above appeared on your list? If more than half did, then you have a pretty good sense of what you can ask for. Hopefully, though, you discovered a few new perks to request in your next job negotiation.

I know from the reaction I get during my negotiating seminar that some of these perks may seem farfetched. But let me assure you that there's not one item that someone who's been fired hasn't negotiated for and gotten going INTO her new position.

Now I'm not suggesting that you ask for all, or even a majority, of the items. Instead, use the master list as a reference guide in considering all your options.

But I'm getting ahead of myself here. First, let's walk through the five steps that will lead up to your actual negotiations:

STEP ONE:
Realistically Assess the Industry, the Complexion of the Company, and the Level of the Position for Which You're Aiming.

Is it a by-the-book, policy-ridden industry or one that has lots of bells and whistles and a reputation for generous perks? Are you going into a small family business where policy can be decided upon on the spot or a large, highly structured corporation? Are you negotiating for a staff position, a middle-management spot, or a top executive post? You need to answer these questions *before* you begin negotiations so that you have a good sense of what your options are.

STEP TWO:
Sit Down with the Master List and Check Off Any Items That You Feel Are Absolute Musts.

And I mean MUSTS—the ones that, if not offered, might keep you from accepting the job. These should be on your A list. Now, factoring your A perks in, calculate the lowest base salary you would accept.

STEP THREE:
Create a B List.

Choose two or three of the remaining perks you'd love to have but you would be willing to give up in a negotiation.

STEP FOUR:
Write Both A and B Perks on a Piece of Paper That You Will Bring with You into Your Negotiating Sessions.

After all, when you go into any sort of a business meeting, you come prepared with notes; a negotiation shouldn't be any different, especially since your anxiety level will be higher here and you don't want to forget anything on your list. What's more, bringing a prepared list could add to an image of professionalism and emphasize your organizational skills.

STEP FIVE:
Rehearse How You Will Ask for Each Item on Your List.

You can't just say "I want luggage." Remember, negotiations aren't about demands but about your ability to sell your ideas in a convincing manner, clearly explaining why a given negotiating issue is in everyone's best interest.

An effective negotiator turns "I want luggage" into "It's been my experience from traveling extensively in other jobs that even though I buy the strongest luggage possible, I go through one or two sets a year. Since there's nothing more unprofessional-looking than arriving at that early morning appointment with a rope tied around a broken piece of luggage, my past company's policy was to reimburse me for my business luggage. I would like to reach a similar agreement here."

No matter what you're negotiating for, keep in mind these three words: "attitude," "attitude," "attitude." Because attitude is your most important asset at this point in the negotiation process; it will either land you the job or send you back to square one. And the most effective attitude is one of confidence—tempered, of course, by an open and flexible negotiating posture.

Now I realize that since you've been let go, feeling and projecting a sense of confidence isn't exactly your strong suit. But if you want to feel more empowered going into your negotiations, remember that at the time you're made an offer you are management's number-one, prime candidate; the one the company really wants. The firm sees you as the solution to its most immediate need. For the moment, you're in the driver's seat—a fact that should bolster your self-esteem.

The Negotiation Itself:
Ten Practical Steps

Before we go through my step-by-step negotiating plan, note these important guidelines. First, never open real negotiations until you've received a formal offer. It's presumptuous and won't be looked upon favorably by your potential new employer.

Second, if you are being pressured to negotiate and accept a job too quickly—and by that I mean on the first interview—be careful. Ask for at least one day to think it over; if that's not acceptable to the new firm, something's fishy. If it is acceptable, then go home, look over your master negotiating list, and prepare yourself.

In most cases, though, you will be made an offer after or during the second, third, or even fourth interview. Make sure you come to these meetings prepared. Remember, though, to let the company make the offer before you bring out your negotiating list. It might be a good idea, just so you won't look too pushy as you reach for your notes, to say something like, "I felt really good after our last interview and was hoping you would offer me the job. So I gave it a good deal of thought and would like to discuss a few points with you."

STEP ONE:
Bring Your A and B Lists with You When You Begin to Negotiate.

Combine them into one list, though; you don't want to tip anyone off about your priorities by shuffling from one list to another.

STEP TWO:
Ask for Clarification Regarding Any Parts of the Opening Offer that You Do Not Fully Understand.

For instance, if you're in sales, make sure you comprehend how your commission will be calculated.

STEP THREE:
State Which Parts of the Offer Are Acceptable to You and
Which Are Not.

Then explain what you need in order for you to accept the position.

You might say, for instance, "I think the base salary is fine and I have no problem with the company's benefit package. But there are a few things that I'd like to open up for discussion. One is that there's been no mention of an expense account and since I will be traveling at least 30 percent of the time, it's important for me to have a company credit card and separate phone charge."

Note that you should speak as if you have the job and are already part of the company. This will convey a strong sense of confidence.

STEP FOUR:
Once You've Stated All That You Want and Listened to the
Counteroffer, Be Prepared to Stick to Your Guns for Those A List
Items, but Show Your Flexibility by Giving Up Something(s)
from Your B List.

Say, for instance, that you really don't care if the company pays for your travel club membership. You might say, "I understand that this is a new division with a tight budget, so if I have to, I could forgo travel club memberships. But I really feel that a telephone charge card is essential for me to do business properly."

STEP FIVE:
If You Hit a Snag, Ask the Company to Help You Solve It.

Let's pose a worst-case scenario. You want a telephone charge card and the company simply won't go along with it. If the charge card is one of your essential A list items, you might put the problem back in the company's lap by saying something like, "Is there anything you can suggest that might resolve this charge card problem? What do your other salespeople do?"

STEP SIX:
Before You Consider Signing On, Understand the Issues
You Probably Cannot Negotiate.

You should *never* begin a job without knowing about certain job specifications. In this case, ignorance is not bliss but possible danger. Before you accept any offer, then, make sure you know:

- Your exact responsibilities, in as much detail as possible.
- Starting date.
- The vacation policy.
- When you will be getting your salary reviews.
- The general company benefits package.
- The company goals and objectives and the particular expectations of your position.
- Your operating budget.
- The person to whom you will directly report. (It may not be the individual who interviewed you.)
- Precisely how much travel you will be doing.
- The company's policy on per diem for travel.
- The location of your office. (Ask to see it. You don't want to be surprised when the window office you expected turns out to be an inner office next to the noisy copy machine.)
- The extent of your support staff. (Will you be allowed to add to staffers and/or make any changes?)
- The amount of entertaining you will be doing.
- Where applicable, the reason your predecessor is no longer there.
- Personal days and sick leave.
- The kind of pension plan the company offers. (This is particularly important if you're over 35 and had to give up a good plan at your former firm.)

STEP SEVEN:
Ask for Time to Think the Offer Over.

Once you have all the facts and the negotiations have gone as far as possible, you have to use your sixth sense about asking for a reasonable amount of time to consider the final offer. (What's reasonable? Anywhere from two to five days.) Then, no matter what you're feeling, go home and think it over. Carefully. Remember what I said before: Whatever you accept now will serve as the basis of all future raises and promotions.

STEP EIGHT:
Reject or Accept the Offer with Finesse.

If you decide this position is not for you, then turn it down gracefully. You never know what the future holds, so act professionally at all times.

If you decide to accept the offer, do it with enthusiasm. Then move on to the next step.

STEP NINE:
Get Everything in Writing.

This does not necessarily mean insisting on a contract; writing the company a letter stating your acceptance is fine. But make sure the letter includes the following: job title, start date, responsibilities, base salary and all perks, and a place where a company executive can initial or sign.

STEP TEN:
Write Your Thanks.

Once you accept a position, thank everyone who has helped you, including your personal contacts and recruiters. It's a nice touch to send a note to other executives with whom you've interviewed reposition, and offering your help should you be able to assist them in the future. Very classy.

It's Not a Job
Till Monday Morning

By nature, I'm an optimistic person. And I hate to burst any bubbles even before they're in the air, but each one of the following has happened to a WIN participant *after* she was offered a position and *before* she accepted it:

- The company decided to fill the job from within.
- A freeze was put on all company hiring.
- The "perfect" candidate (sometimes the boss's niece, nephew, or brother-in-law) appeared at the last minute.
- The person who was going to hire you quit or got fired.
- A last-minute reference did not check out well.
- A company takeover threatened the position.

These situations are the exceptions, not the rule. But they happen enough to warrant preparing yourself by not giving up your job search until you have either a written commitment from the company or have actually started the job.

Now, if all this talk about interviewing properly and negotiating effectively has you anxious and fed up, you may be thinking "The hell with this. Maybe I should start my own business." But should you? There's lot to consider here, too, as chapter 10 explains.

10.

If Mary Kay Can Do It, Why Can't You? Starting Your Own Business

All right. You've been fired, maybe not even for the first time. You're fed up with corporate life; you can't bear the thought of reporting to one more jerk. You've been working so hard for so many years, and where has it got you? All you can think is, "I'm not going to let this happen to me again. Why should I work hard so someone else can get rich? If Mary Kay can do it, why can't I? I'm going into business for myself!"

No, I don't have ESP. It's just that most recently fired women I meet confess to having had these thoughts, at least one time or another, since they lost their jobs. So if the same thoughts are running through your mind right now, you're in good company.

Lots of women have not only thought about starting their own businesses, they've done it. The numbers, though reported by a variety of sources, are consistently impressive:

- In 1986, nonfarm (nonagricultural) sole proprietorships owned by women reached 4.1 million—a 62 percent jump from 1980, according to the Small Business Administration (SBA).

- IRS statistics show that women own some 30 percent of American nonfarm sole proprietorships as of 1986.
- As of 1988, women represented 35 percent of all self-employed individuals, reports the Bureau of Labor Statistics. (And, since this figure excludes the incorporated self-employed, the actual percentage of self-employed women is a good deal higher.)
- By the year 2000, women will comprise 50 percent of all self-employed people, according to data reported in the Women's Business Ownership Act of 1988.

Why have such staggering numbers of women been motivated to start their own businesses? Several reasons. One you already know—they've been fired. Job loss and the increasing difficulty in repositioning themselves, particularly in certain shrinking industries and at high levels of management, are prime motivators for women to get out on their own. Another is hitting the "glass ceiling." Women's frustration with the lack of corporate opportunities, combined with their years of hands-on experience operating in the business world, often make entrepreneurship appealing. Many women, especially mothers, are seeking more flexible employment situations than the traditional workplace allows.

Women are also realizing that job security is a thing of the past. Thus, they figure, if you're going to take risks, why not do it for yourself?

Finally, role models such as Mary Kay (cosmetics), Debbie Fields (cookies), Liz Claiborne (apparel), and Lois Wyse (advertising) exemplify what women entrepreneurs can achieve. Today, starting your own business is no longer an impossible dream.

Yet, for many women, it's an improbable one.

Remember those cheerful statistics I listed before? Well, here's another: According to the SBA, nearly one quarter of new companies fail within their first two years. And another: Only four in ten new ventures make it past six years.

The main reasons for such a high rate of failure include undercapitalization, inadequate market research, and misguided partnerships. I also believe that when people start businesses *only* as a knee-jerk reaction to having been fired, they set themselves up for an even greater rate of failure.

Listen to this: A study of entrepreneurs conducted by Joseph R. Mancuso, founder of the New York–based Center for Entrepreneurial Management, showed that most true entrepreneurs will quit their jobs rather than wait around to get fired. Thus, Mancuso's finding raises an interesting question for those of you who *only* considered starting your own business after you were fired: very simply, why did you stay in the corporate world for so long? Your answer may well reveal that what's prompting you to consider entrepreneurship is your current career crisis and not a real desire to go it alone. If that's true for you, I strongly urge you to think long and hard before taking the entrepreneurial option.

Businesses tend to fail when you start them for the wrong reasons. And there are plenty of them, including hating your ex-boss, wanting to make lots of money, being bored with your career, or wanting more free time. All of these can be remedied by finding a new job, company, or career that will offer more of what you want; rest assured that they won't necessarily be satisfied by starting your own business.

The right reasons for starting your own business, says Jeannette Scollard, entrepreneur and author of *The Self-Employed Woman*, "have more to do with your choice of lifestyle. When you really resent 9–5, being cooped up in an office, and having to match your work style to someone else's, then you might want to consider working for yourself."

But even Scollard, who wholeheartedly supports female entrepreneurship, warns in *The Self-Employed Woman*: "Do not act in haste. Becoming an entrepreneur is nothing to rush into. It means you receive no salary, no benefits, no office, and no support system unless you can supply it for yourself. Moreover, when you take the step to start, you are committed to taking certain risks, and whenever there are risks, there is a high potential for failure. Deliberate at length before you decide to go into business for yourself."

What Makes a Woman
an Entrepreneur

When Joseph Mancuso of the Center for Entrepreneurial Management surveyed entrepreneurial men, he found that they showed certain characteristics. In general, they were:

- First-born children.
- Children of an entrepreneur (or entrepreneurs).
- Enterprising. Even as children, they had a paper route, mowed lawns, or found other jobs to earn money. As Mancuso explains: "While every kid who runs a lemonade stand won't necessarily grow up to be an entrepreneur; a kid who runs a chain of lemonade stands is a good bet."
- Well educated. Most of the entrepreneurs surveyed had a bachelor's degree, and many an M.B.A.
- Married, with supportive mates.

Subsequent research, such as that reported by Hisrich and Brush in *The Woman Entrepreneur*, reveals that entrepreneurial women share these characteristics. In addition, they tend to be older (thirty-five to forty-five years of age for women, as opposed to thirty to thirty-five years of age for men) when they start their own businesses. Also, Hisrich and Brush report, women entrepreneurs tend to be married to men earning more than $50,000 a year, which reduces their financial anxiety.

Over the last several years, I've met lots of women who own and operate their own businesses, and I've noticed that they share several personality traits. That's not to say that men don't have them as well, but since my observations are based on women, I've come up with a profile of the female entrepreneur based on twenty common characteristics.

Twenty Typical Traits
of the Female Entrepreneur

(1) RISK-TAKING
Going out on your own is risky business. It means giving up the security of a steady paycheck and chancing possible failure. Yet while entrepreneurs are willing to take risks, they don't do so recklessly, and they tend to weigh the odds before making any major moves.

(2) DECISION-MAKING
Entrepreneurs are able to assimilate information and make clear, confident decisions quickly. If you tend to be a fence-sitter, then going it alone isn't for you.

(3) INDEPENDENCE
Entrepreneurial women don't tend to stick around the corporate world for long—and for good reason. They don't like working for other people, prefer to do things their own way, and feel happiest when they are in command.

(4) CREATIVITY, INNOVATIVENESS, RESOURCEFULNESS
Being entrepreneurial means thinking on your feet. Successful self-employed women are adept at finding creative solutions to whatever problems arise—from locating the best suppliers to publicizing their product to generating customers.

(5) FLEXIBILITY, ADAPTABILITY
To paraphrase Robert Burns, even the best laid business plans often go awry, so entrepreneurs learn to remain flexible and open-minded at all times.

(6) MOTIVATION
Highly motivated, entrepreneurs are self-starters—able to get themselves and their projects going without any outside prodding.

(7) HIGH ENERGY LEVELS

It takes a good deal of physical and emotional stamina to start and maintain a business.

(8) DISCIPLINE

Entrepreneurs exercise self-control and don't let themselves get distracted from their goals. They maintain their self-discipline not just for long-term objectives but on a day-to-day basis as well.

(9) ORGANIZATION

Make that a capital "O" for Organization. Self-employed women keep their affairs in order, make lots of lists, and stick to them. They're also great planners.

(10) MULTIPLE TALENTS

Months after I started my own business I had a revelation: In corporate America, you get paid to do one thing really well. But when you start your own business, you have to do everything well, from making cold calls to marketing your product to balancing the books. Which is why many entrepreneurs are either multitalented or are adept at finding others whose strengths make up for their weaknesses.

(11) CONFIDENCE

Entrepreneurs have solid self-confidence and the ability to project that confidence to others.

(12) EFFECTIVE LEADER/MANAGER ABILITIES

Entrepreneurs are take-charge people who inspire, motivate, and elicit loyalty from their staffs. They also know how and when to delegate authority.

(13) HIGH RESPONSIBILITY

You'd be hard-pressed to find an irresponsible entrepreneur, mainly because without a strong sense of responsibility and accountability she'd be out of business before she could say, well, "Entrepreneur."

(14) OPTIMISM
Obstacles become opportunities to self-employed women. They don't just make lemonade out of lemons; they use the leftover rinds to make lemon cookies, muffins, and tarts.

(15) PERSEVERANCE
Entrepreneurs don't give up easily. They work hard—a National Association of Women Business Owners survey showed these women average sixty- to eighty-hour work weeks—and keep going, no matter what problems arise. At least to a point. Because an entrepreneur is also savvy and knows when to cut her losses.

(16) ENTHUSIASM
An entrepreneur is enthusiastic by nature. In particular, she tends to be turned on by the excitement and risk of a start-up situation, but she may become bored once the business gets rolling. Then she moves on to the next opportunity.

(17) ORIENTATION TO GOALS
Self-employed women set both short- and long-term goals and do whatever is necessary to meet them. But being realistic (see number 19), they readjust their goals whenever necessary.

(18) ORIENTATION TO PEOPLE
Many would-be entrepreneurs believe that working for yourself means working alone. But that's just not so. When you're in your own business, you have to be equally comfortable and effective dealing with everyone from presidents of companies to the telephone repair person.

(19) REALISM
While entrepreneurs are optimistic, enthusiastic, and confident, they never lose their objectivity. They periodically assess and reassess their business dealings and objectives, based on their firm grasp of reality.

(20) COMPETITIVENESS

The desire to excel drives entrepreneurs toward their goals. It's what makes them strive to be better than their competitors.

I believe these characteristics shape the personality of the "classic" female entrepreneur. Of course, you don't have to possess all of them to be successful. But if reading this list made you say "That's me" more often than not, then you may have what it takes to go into business for yourself.

WIN's Twenty-Minute Guide to Starting Your Own Business

If you're really serious about starting your own business, there are numerous books, courses, and organizations whose sole purpose it is to inform and guide you on your entrepreneurial journey. You need this education; don't skimp on it. I recommend several valuable resources in the bibliography.

Among your first moves, though, should be to call the Answer Desk—1-800-368-5855—a toll-free hot line set up by the Small Business Administration to answer any questions you may have regarding starting your own business. The hot line will also refer you to the nearest SBA office for further information.

My main intention in this chapter, however, is to offer those of you who have not yet made the commitment to become self-employed a quick sampling of what's involved. If you fall into that category, then peruse WIN's Twenty-Minute Guide to Starting Your Own Business.

THE VIABLE IDEA/MARKET RESEARCH

Often, the idea for a business begins as an answer to a personal need. For instance, my friend Sharon started a company when she noticed that her toddler's disposable diaper kept hanging out of her bathing suit. So Sharon designed a line of swimsuits contoured to cover kids' diapers.

217

Then there's my friend Sue. When her daughter was applying to college, Sue became upset by the lack of guidance and information provided by the high school counselor. So she launched a service business that helps other confused parents and high school students research their best options for higher education.

Both of these businesses became quite successful, but neither did so by chance. Each woman not only worked hard but also did her homework, identifying her potential customers and then testing their response to the particular product or service to be offered. In other words, they did some essential market research.

Bear in mind that just because your sister Diane says she'd order a dozen of whatever you're selling doesn't mean the rest of the world will, too. You need to test-market your business idea thoroughly *before* investing too much of your resources.

There are lots of ways to test-market effectively, and again, if you're really serious about it, I urge you to read some of the books in the bibliography and at your local library and to contact your local SBA. But let me touch on some of the basics.

First, check out the competition—what they charge, what you will offer that they don't, and why you'll be better. Next, if your business is product oriented, make up a prototype. Then figure out how much it would cost you to produce it in quantity. Make sure you include your production costs, materials, labor, overhead, promotion, *and* profit.

Take the prototype to your potential customers. These could be consumers, local retailers who would buy from you at wholesale and sell to the consumer at retail, or whoever else you feel is your target audience. Listen to what they have to say. Do they need the product? Would they buy it at the price at which you want to sell it? When would they buy it (many items are seasonal)? And how many might they order?

Now suppose you've developed an idea for a service business. Print up a flyer and/or take an ad in a local publication in which you offer your services. Then see if you get any bites.

Another way to test-market your product or idea is to get a group of people together (not your good friends; you want objective opinions now) and run an informal focus group during which you ask for comments on the viability of your business.

I should say here that there are professional market research firms who will do all this for you on a much more sophisticated level, but they are very expensive. If you have the commitment and the resources, though, perhaps you should consider such firms. But if you're working on a tight budget, give it a go yourself.

THE "MIDPRENEUR" AND FRANCHISING OPTIONS

In the cases of Sue, Sharon, and many others, an original, viable idea developed into a real business. But what if you want to be self-employed and don't have an innovative idea or aren't comfortable taking big risks? Then you have two other options: becoming a "midpreneur" (a term coined by Robert and Madeleine Swain in their book *Out the Organization*) or buying a franchise.

According to the Swains, "an entrepreneur is a risk taker, totally and completely. He or she creates the business idea, develops it, brings it to fruition, and reaps the rewards—or suffers the losses. . . . The midpreneur, although stepping out from under the protective corporate canopy, will perhaps adapt an existing idea, or continue to expand a business found to be successful."

Central to midpreneurship is lessening the risk. A midpreneur, for example, might start her own advertising firm but specialize in publicizing health spas. Or she might open a bed and breakfast (or buy an existing one) in her hometown.

If midpreneurism doesn't appeal to you, there's another option: the franchise. When you buy a franchise—for example, a McDonald's or Century 21—you really buy a partner and a company name. As Jeannette Scollard says in *The Self-Employed Woman*: "With a franchise, your chances of succeeding are better because you are not in the position of reinventing the wheel. Your business has already been thought through for you, so there is less you need to learn the hard way. The franchise trains you, helps you, answers your questions, and generally tells you how to run a successful business."

ON YOUR OWN OR WITH A PARTNER

Whether or not to go into business all by yourself or to work with a partner is one of the first business decisions you'll have to make. There's no right or wrong answer; you must decide this one all on your own.

Going solo means you get to make all the decisions, work at your own pace, reap the financial rewards, and take the credit if the business succeeds. But as the song goes, one is the loneliest number, particularly if you're used to the social ambiance of corporate America. You won't have anyone to bounce ideas off, share financial risks with, or help grow the business.

The advantages of working with a partner include sharing the workload and financial responsibility. A partner can (and should) also supply the expertise you lack in a given area, assist in generating additional business, help shoulder the burden, and share the joy.

The downside of partnerships involves having to live with another person's ego and idiosyncrasies, sharing the profits, having someone else to answer to, needing to get another person's input before you can make certain decisions, and having conflicting ideas about where the company's going and how it should be getting there. You may feel taken advantage of by a partner who you perceive is not carrying her share of the workload, and/or you may disagree about how money should be spent. While often workable—even preferable for some—partnerships are not as simple as many women think.

Anna Riback-Gibson learned that life-lesson well. After she was fired from her position as president of a commercial drapery workroom in Chicago, she says, "I licked my wounds for a few months and talked about it with lots of friends." One of those friends was Judy O'Brien.

Remembers Anna: "My son was away at camp; hers was at college. One day, I got a flyer in the mail advertising camp care packages (ready-made packages of special goodies parents can send to their kids in camp), and we thought, 'Why not college care packages?' "

Anna and Judy headed for a few local campuses to find out whether there was a need for such packages, and the answer was an unqualified yes. Encouraged, they started checking out vendors and wholesalers and came up with five creative "college care packages" that launched their new mail-order company, *Send-Sational.*

Before they invested a great deal in the firm, they ran a test, hand-stuffing "thousands of envelopes" with a mailer they sent to college kids' parents. The test, says Anna, "was very successful," and the business, officially launched in the fall of 1988, was on its way. Today, the company offers a wide assortment of wonderful care packages—including "Emotional Rescue" (a Slinky, rubber chicken, happy-face mask, animal nose, yo-yo, etc.) and "In the Midnight Hour" (microwaveable pasta-and-cheese dinner, cereal snack packs, potato chips, giant chocolate chip cookies)—and Anna is confident that the business will not just survive but flourish.

Yet, she admits, "the hardest part for me has been the partnership. For a time, it was really difficult because we are both independent professionals as well as friends. And when interpersonal problems came up, we *had* to work them out because our friendship was now part of our business—how we felt affected our company.

"What I learned from the experience is that when you go into business with a partner, especially if she's also a friend, all her (or his) little idiosyncrasies come out. And you have to deal with that.

"Also, though our individual strengths and weaknesses complemented each other, they made us lock horns a lot. I'm very detail oriented and analytical; Judy's very action oriented, creative, and has these short-term bursts of energy. Which means that we approach things very differently. When we had to write the copy for our brochure, we had very different ideas about what to say to our potential customers and how to say it. And that's just one example.

"For a partnership to work, you have to stay open-minded, even though your tendency, your first inclination, is to say 'I'm right and you're wrong.' "

Despite the problems, though, women still tend to favor partnerships. They tend to want the security and sociability of a partnership and often lack the self-confidence they need to believe they can make it completely on their own. Also, women believe that a partnership will give them more flexibility—if one partner has a doctor's appointment, or a sick child at home, the other can cover for her.

I know that when I first conceived of WIN Workshops, I tried to convince my friend Wendy to become my partner. After many meetings, she decided it wasn't for her, and in retrospect, her decision turned out to be right for us both. But it took me a long time to feel comfortable and confident as the sole proprietor of a new venture.

UNEXPECTED AND HIDDEN COSTS

Businesses often cost more to launch than you think. You have to pay for insurance (medical, liability, and insurance on your equipment and inventory), office supplies, a computer, a typewriter, a facsimile machine, a business telephone (line installation, the phone system itself, monthly bills), office rent, legal and accounting services, an answering machine or service, postage, equipment maintenance, letterhead, business cards, advertising and graphic design services, Social Security taxes, and incorporation or sole partnership fees, not to mention the cost of borrowing money. You may also need certain licenses or permits to start your business; check with a local government agency to find out what you will need and how much it will cost.

Even a service business you set up in your home has overhead. Take Nancy Smith's venture, for instance. For several years, she had worked for a real estate firm in Arizona. After she was let go, she decided to open up her own real estate firm. But it wasn't quite as easy as she had anticipated; unexpected and hidden costs kept mounting.

"First, I tried to work out of my home, but I wasn't disciplined enough to leave the dishes and go to my desk. So after three months, I had to rent office space. Though I share it with a friend, it's still a cost I didn't anticipate. Then, there are those other expenses: board fees, license fees, forms, office furniture, office supplies, an answering machine, the leasing fees for a computer, the MLS (multiple listing books), and advertising."

Eighteen months after going out on her own, Nancy is doing well enough to be optimistic about her business's long-term prospects. But she offers this advice to anyone just starting out: "When you start your own business, you need some money in the bank. You have to be able to cover your business expenses and your personal ones. Remember, you don't make money right away and you have to be prepared for that."

Some experts say that you should be prepared and able to live for one or two years without drawing any income from your business. This is a great guideline for someone who has seriously planned to start a business for a long time and has had adequate time to save up for it. But if you've only thought or talked about it and it's your firing that has propelled you into action, then you might not have an adequate financial base or the time to build one. In that case, I often advise would-be entrepreneurs to get a job and start saving their money. Ideally, that job should be with a company in the same or related field as your intended business so that you can learn on its time.

FINANCING

Many, if not most, businesses fail because they are undercapitalized. People tend to underestimate just how much cash they'll need to get their businesses going and see them grow.

To figure out how much you'll need, and then to seek the financial backing necessary, you'll have to develop a business plan that will include the following things.

- A concise definition and summary of your business.
- A profile of the competitive marketplace.
- Your goals for the company.
- Marketing and production plans.
- Profiles of your company principals.
- Your estimated income and expenses (the company's cash flow).
- A break-even analysis.

- The amount and purpose of your loan.
- How you plan to pay back the loan.
- What collateral you can offer.

Pulling all this information together can be rather complex—too complex, in fact, to deal with in this twenty-minute guide. So once again, if you're serious about starting your own business, I suggest you call the SBA Answer Desk, consult with an accountant and/or a lawyer, and spend some time in a good business library. As a jumping-off point, check the bibliography of this book.

Various financial resources can help you get started in business. Most women think of banks first, and it's true that they do finance many new ventures. But beware; sexism still exists in these institutions, particularly when it comes to borrowing money.

If you do get turned down for a loan, it may be because you've presented insufficient financial information. In fact, the SBA says that this is the main reason new entrepreneurs get a thumbs-down from the bank. If you get a no, a smart follow-up tactic is to ask the bank for a Small Business Administration Guarantee, by which, essentially, the SBA guarantees repayment of your loan. This move could get you the bank funds you need.

You should also know about the Women's Business Ownership Act of 1988, which, among other things, opened up avenues for women to get access to capital and credit. Check with the Small Business Administration in your area or in Washington for more information.

Other than banks, you can use your own assets and savings or those of your family, or turn to friends, private investors, or venture capitalists to finance your business.

HELPFUL OTHERS

Even when you're going into business without any partners, you can't do it totally alone. There are times when you'll need others with particular professional expertise. This is another expense you'll need to anticipate. These "others" can include the following professionals:

A Lawyer

You'll need to comply with lots of rules and regulations, so often a lawyer will be an invaluable help. Legal assistance may also be necessary when doing such things as signing contracts, incorporating, or, heaven forbid, handling any litigation that may arise.

An Accountant

Even if you're a great numbers person, you may need the services of an accountant to help you with the financial details of your firm or, if nothing else, to help prepare your taxes.

An Insurance Agent

Businesses and the people who own them (and work for them) need insurance, so hook yourself up with a trustworthy insurance agent before you open your doors.

A Banker

Choose a banker carefully and then be sure to make friends with him or her. A good banker may be able to cut through some of the red tape that often entangles a novice entrepreneur seeking financing.

A Business Consultant

Occasionally you may need to hire an outside consultant to solve a one-time problem. For instance, you may want to hire someone to help you write your business plan, run a market test on your product, test the location of your retail operation, or design an effective production system.

Creative Consultants.

Your company may need the services of a creative consultant for such tasks as designing a company logo, writing your sales brochure, or publicizing you or your company.

To find the right "helpful others" for you, use the same techniques you would to find a good doctor, dentist, or even interior decorator. First, rely on word of mouth; a personal reference from someone you respect is always an excellent way to find a competent professional. Also, check professional associations. The local Bar Association, for instance, will be helpful in finding an accredited lawyer. And don't forget to shop around. It's perfectly acceptable to speak with two, three, or more professionals until you find the one who best suits your needs.

MARKETING/PROMOTING/ADVERTISING/SELLING

For the purpose of my twenty-minute guide, I've decided to lump together these four topics because essentially they revolve around one key process—exposing your product or service to potential customers. The purpose: to explain what it is you're selling and just how it will serve your clientele. Here are some of the things involved:

Developing a Company Image
Figure out your company's identity, that is, what image you want to convey. For instance, Tiffany & Co. has worked for years to create and sustain an upscale image; the firm is known for the finest quality products. K mart represents another end of the spectrum; its customers know that K mart stands for value.

Logo Trademark
Once you've defined your image, it's time to create your company's logo, which can incorporate anything from a particular typeface (like the Coca-Cola logo), to a specific color (my friend Barbara uses purple for everything from company pens to letterhead), to a specially designed graphic (such as the CBS eye or McDonald's' golden arches).

Once you've got your logo, use it! Put it on your business cards, stationery, invoices, mailing pieces, trucks, company cars, packaging, labels—everything. You need to create a consistent image so that anyone who spots your logo will immediately think of your company.

One essential point: *Before* you spend lots of money on a company name, logo, or special graphics, make sure that it's unique and doesn't infringe on someone else's (or another company's) identity. You may want to speak with local business associations or the Small Business Administration about such things as a D.B.A. (doing business as), as well as copyrights and trademarks to preserve and protect your company name and logo. In some cases, you might need the services of a lawyer.

Don't ignore this issue; it's a common pitfall for beginning entrepreneurs. In fact, it's been known to cause more than a few gray hairs on the heads of experienced businesspersons. A while back, my collaborator wrote a book about the founding of a major East Coast supermarket chain. In her research, she heard a story that illustrates the perils of adopting a logo all too well. I'll let her tell it:

"A group of supermarket entrepreneurs had decided to launch their own chain of food stores. They came up with the name Pathway and even developed the now-famous red-and-blue logo design. In order to meet certain interstate commerce regulations, they had to have the logo printed on the first product cans, cans of soda, on a Tuesday. Well, everything was set to go, when on the Thursday before, one of the founders opened up a local newspaper and saw an ad for Pathway Products! Pathway turned out to be some sort of door-to-door cleaning supplies firm that already had a copyright on the name. To make that Tuesday soda can deadline, the panicked founders brainstormed permutations of the name, but everything they thought of was already taken. Finally, they came up with a nonword that they knew would not have been used, which, in a nutshell, is how Pathmark got its name. But can you imagine the cost the fledgling firm would have incurred, not to mention the potential lawsuits and incredible embarrassment if they had not seen that newspaper ad and gone with their original name?"

Enough said. Learn from others' mistakes, and be sure to check your name, logo, or trademark out *before* proceeding.

Advertising

The difference between advertising and publicity is simple: You pay for the former; the latter is free. Advertising can range from placing an ad in the Yellow Pages to printing out a flyer on a home computer and distributing it, to running an ad in a local paper, to taking out a full-color ad in a national magazine or buying a one-minute spot on network TV.

Advertising can be extremely expensive; national advertising can be prohibitive, particularly for a start-up venture. So start small, move slowly, and pick your spots carefully based upon thorough analysis of the medium's target audience and its ability to reach your customers cost-effectively.

If you're planning to use an advertising agency, be prepared to pay handsomely. Also be aware that many won't even bother with a small client. An alternative would be to hire an individual consultant on a project basis. Again, personal referral is an excellent way to find such an expert.

Publicity

Getting your (and your company's) name to the public's attention for free involves a lot of footwork on your part. For instance, you could start attending local chamber of commerce meetings and become more involved in community activities. This will build your personal credibility and, thus, your company's. You could try to give speeches at local organizations, write a column for the newspapers, or stage newsworthy, company-related events to get local press coverage. It's often a good idea to develop a press kit. This should include a brief bio of you (and other company principals), a description of your product or service, testimonials, appropriate photographs, and, as you get more publicity, news clips about you and your firm. A press kit can be elaborate or fairly simple, but it should always look clean and professional. Mail the kit to whomever you feel might give you some free publicity, such as trade publications, local newspapers, and local radio and TV programs.

The most effective way to target good publicity sources is to use a good directory; one of the most popular is Bacon's Publicity

Checker. There's one for TV, another for radio, and a third for print, including newspapers and magazines, and they are available in selected libraries or directly from the publisher.

If you have the money, you might consider hiring a professional public relations company or an individual consultant to put the word out there for you. Just make sure that their connections are good in your field.

Consumer Brochure/Direct Mail

You may want to consider some sort of direct-mail piece, perhaps a brochure or a simple postcard mailer announcing and/or promoting your company, product, or service. In situations where your company's potential client base is fairly specific—say, new homeowners, brides, dog lovers, retirees, dentists—direct mail is often more cost-effective than other forms of advertising, because it enables you to reach *only* those consumers who fit your customer profile.

But just because you send out one thousand mailers doesn't mean you'll get one thousand or even five hundred responses. Consider yourself doing fine if you get fifteen answers. You should expect to get a response rate of 1 to 2 percent on any direct mailing you do.

While this guide may only take twenty minutes to read, setting up your own business can (and probably will) take months. But don't get discouraged. For some inspiration, here are the personal stories of two women who've experienced the pitfalls and pleasures of having their own business.

Laura's Story: Worldly Treasures

Laura Baldasare was fired from her position as director of purchasing when new management decided to bring in its own team. "I foundered around for a while, sent my résumé around, but nothing that I was interested in came up. To be honest, I also didn't *want* to go back to corporate. I had been there for twelve years, but inside I always rebelled. I don't like being told what to do; I know I excel when I'm allowed to be independent.

"Luckily, my husband was able to carry us financially, so I wasn't under great financial pressure. Then one day, a woman I had met through some committee work stopped by for coffee. We talked for several hours and that very day, decided to go into business together."

Now they had to decide what kind of business to try. As Laura says: "My background was international—in purchasing, marketing, and finance. Her interest was in mail order. So we decided to start a jewelry mail-order firm."

Fortunately, the women well understood that mail order can be costly. "I knew we'd need about a half a million to start, so before we plunged in, we did a very careful test, investing $5,000 each of our own money to bring in a few pieces of product, create a four-color flyer, print up a cover letter and order forms, and run a few classified ads in women's magazines."

The test yielded some important information: "Fine jewelry just doesn't lend itself to mail order, especially when you don't have a well-known name," says Laura. "Over the course of four or five months we got only three hundred inquiries and no orders."

So Laura and her partner decided to shift gears and revamp their original idea. "We decided to stay with jewelry, but go with a less expensive line and stick to importing, not direct mail. Called Worldly Treasures Ltd., our company now imports product and sells it directly to jewelry stores. And it's doing very well," Laura says.

She is quick to admit, however, that keeping the business healthy is a constant struggle. "At this point, we're just breaking even, and we're still not drawing a salary. But I'm hopeful that next year, we will.

"You know, you don't go into your own business for the money. And sure, there were times during that first year that I thought about going back to corporate. But you can't beat the independence and flexibility of having your own business. I've very happy having my own business, but let's face it. It's a lot of plain, hard work!"

Suzanne's Story: My Perfect Partner

When artist Suzanne Kiefer was told by the heads of the advertising agency she worked for that she would not be promoted because she "had no business or managerial skills," she decided she'd had enough of corporate life. So she chose to start her own business based on a unique idea—manufacturing satin sheets imprinted with a life-size, full-color picture of a bikini-underwear-clad man. Within several months, her company, Multiply By Two, introduced a line of man-adorned satin bed linens called My Perfect Partner. Today, she and her company are alive and exceedingly well. But getting the business off the ground was far from easy, Suzanne recalls.

"First, I kept my job at the ad agency and took on two free-lance art jobs to make as much money as I possibly could, all the while getting my business going 'on the side.' During this time, I went to the library, researched, and talked to manufacturing companies and as many other sources as I could to investigate the printing process, the costs, the textile industry." Then, as the business started to roll, Suzanne went solo.

By the second year she had invested about $120,000 of her own money in the firm. But Suzanne soon learned that being in business for herself carried an emotional as well as a financial price tag. She says: "You have to be able to give up everything for your company. You don't see friends, relationships get shaky, there's no time for family, or for sleep for that matter. I have my nails done at 7:30 A.M. because it's the only time I have.

"You also learn that you have to be willing to do everything yourself. My first year, just before Christmas, I had to personally refold and repackage eight hundred sheets because the company I had hired to do it botched up the job. Oh, and I also had to learn about invoicing, shipping, and lots of other things.

"And another thing. When you have your own business, you work twice as hard, and initially for less money, than you ever did before. I'm entering my third year and I still don't take a salary. And I've only just moved the company out of my home and into a real office. But the company is growing strong and I know we'll be turning a profit by the end of this year."

Despite the many difficulties, Suzanne is confident that becoming an entrepreneur was right for her. As she says: "I realized that I have to be on my own. I have to be in control and I love to make things happen. I already have two other businesses I'm planning to start. And you know what? Now, people are coming to me with their ideas for a business. Me, the one who supposedly had 'no business sense.' And I really love it!"

By now my message should be pretty clear: Starting your own business is a lot more complex than you might have realized. And while it's great for some, it's not for everybody.

If you've decided it's not for you (at least right now), then you'll soon be returning to the corporate world, particularly if you utilize all the strategies offered in the previous chapters.

Yet the story doesn't end here. There's one final chapter, and it's an absolute MUST for every working woman.

11.

Congratulations! You've Been Hired; Now, Plan On Being Fired

Let's assume that by now you've landed a new job, at least for the purposes of this chapter. After all, if you've researched, networked, interviewed, and negotiated, using the tactics outlined in the earlier chapters, how could you miss!

But before you get too comfortable in your new niche, however wonderful it might be, remember that in today's economy, job security is a thing of the past. No one knows better than you that anyone can be fired and at any time. So plan for it . . . now.

When you think about it, we plan for things all the time. We do long-term planning—where we'll go on vacation, whom we'll go with, which airline, what flight. And we plan for the short-term—when to start the coffee perking so it will be ready after our morning shower, what to wear to the office, when to fill the car with gas. If you have any doubts about how much planning you do every day, just check out your appointment book—9:30 meeting with Jane, 10:30 production meeting, noon lunch with prospective client, 2:30 proposal deadline, 3:30 conference with printer.

Why do we plan so much? Because we feel more comfortable when we're able to control, or at least reasonably anticipate, what's going to happen. Planning gives structure to our daily lives. As psychologist Marilyn Puder-York explains: "Structure implies predictability, a certain stability and security. And it also gives most people a certain sense of control over their lives. We all need a certain amount of regularity in our lives—an organizing principle."

Organizing principle notwithstanding, though, the one thing that can turn your life topsy-turvy—those two little words "You're fired"— is the one thing we never plan for. So let's change that. Right now, while you're sitting pretty at your new job, it's time to *plan on being fired*.

Keep Your Perspective

First of all, don't get trapped in the old habit of making the job your home, of settling in and thinking it's going to last forever. After all, you may decide to leave voluntarily because (1) you've found a better position (2) you're ready to make a career change, or (3) you've decided to work for yourself. Or, you could be fired again.

Not that you shouldn't invest lots of energy in your new post; certainly, do the best job you can do. But if your office starts looking more like your living room than your workplace, it's time to step back and take stock. An even better approach is to be smart right from the start and put everything into its proper perspective.

Network—Again!

When you start a new job, the tendency, especially after you've experienced a firing and need to rebuild self-esteem, is to go back to the same old way of doing business and give yourself over completely to your job: getting to the office early, eating at your desk, leaving late, not taking any time out to maintain your connections. But this is another trap that you can easily avoid by networking—again.

If you've followed the advice in chapter 7, you've made a lot of new, wonderful contacts, both in and out of your industry. Hopefully, you've also rekindled some professional and personal friendships. DON'T LET THEM GO!

You know how you feel when someone *only* calls every two or three years to say, "Guess what? I'm out of work again and need your help?" You feel used and really don't want to lend a hand, right? Well, neither will your contacts if they rarely hear from you. So put yourself in their shoes and maintain the network that you've built up.

To begin, make a list of twenty to forty people with whom you can touch base. They should be strictly professional contacts, such as former suppliers or employers, or friendly former co-workers and colleagues, anyone but friends you usually chat with regularly. Put each name (with its corresponding phone number) on an index card.

Then take ten minutes every day, whether first thing in the morning or late in the afternoon—whatever time fits your schedule best—and call one or two persons in your new card file to maintain that contact.

You don't have to spend a long time on the phone. Actually, if you're in your office, you shouldn't. But all it takes is something brief and simple like, "Hi, this new job has got me tied to my desk. I don't have time to have even a cup of coffee, let alone lunch, but I wanted you to know I was thinking about you and wondered how you are."

After each call, note the date and anything newsworthy to follow up on next time you speak (such as your contact's daughter's wedding or upcoming vacation to China). Then put the card at the end of the file until you've gone through the entire list and are ready to begin again.

The point is: *Don't isolate yourself.* Don't wait until it's too late and you have to call all those people all over again and say, "Guess what?" So plan this telephone networking—put it right into your appointment book—and don't miss a single day.

As I've said before, networking works, but only if you do it.

Write Your Thanks

If you haven't done it by now, sit down and write a thank-you note to anyone and everyone who helped you in your job search. Whether it was a colleague who actually connected you with your new company or a friend who lent an ear, send a few words to those you feel were genuinely thoughtful, caring, and helpful.

I know you're busy settling into your new job and you feel as if you don't have the time to do anything extra. (Ironic, isn't it, after having had so much time on your hands?) But writing a few notes each evening won't take up much time, and the long-term payoff (in nurturing your contacts) will be well worth the effort.

Be a Joiner

Now is also the time to join, or renew your membership in, professional groups. As I suggested in chapter 7, start thinking outside of your field as well. You probably attend professional functions or meetings in your own industry with someone you already know (so you don't meet many new people) and discuss topics you already understand well. This doesn't give you the opportunity to broaden your horizons and meet other people who have nothing to do with your job.

It's very exciting for a copywriter in an advertising agency to meet people who are in catering, animal training, or talent management. Getting to know people who have chosen other career paths can inspire you to start thinking in new, broader directions whether you stay in your current line of work or not.

For instance, the caterer you met recently may need someone to copywrite a sales brochure on a free-lance basis. Or her ex-husband may be starting up a small new video marketing agency and is looking for someone to head up the scriptwriting department. The more people you meet, and the more you talk to those people you meet, the more people you'll meet.

Avoiding the Money Crunch:
The Career Crisis Club

No one has to tell you what a financial crunch being fired can cause, and it's a safe bet that you don't want to go through THAT again. So plan to avoid it *now*.

Banks are onto a good idea. They've set up Christmas Clubs, which are really nothing more than forced savings plans that prepare you for Christmas spending sprees.

So steal their idea and set up a Career Crisis Club. You should figure that a job hunt will take one month of searching for every $10,000 you used to earn; it could well take you months to find a satisfactory new position. For example, if you're making $40,000, it might take you three to four months to replace your job. (Don't panic; this is an *average* figure. However, even though it could take you two weeks, it might also take the full four months or more to find the right position.)

Now you can use this measure to calculate just how much money you'll need to weather any impending financial storm. For instance, if it will take you six months to get a new job—remember, this is an approximation, not a guarantee—you will need six months' worth of expenses put away in a bank savings account, money market, or some other SAFE investment. It's a good idea to make sure this money is relatively liquid so that you can get at the cash easily in a crisis.

Now let's do some more figuring.

Write down your essential or fixed monthly expenses, such as rent, food, utilities, transportation, insurance, loan payments. Put an estimated amount next to each.

Then write down your nonessential or flexible expenses, including the gym, manicures, facials, clothing, entertainment, gifts. Again, put the amount you usually spend each month next to each.

Total your fixed expenses, then multiply that number by the number of months you can expect to be unemployed (that's one month for each $10,000 you earned in your last job).

If you need some help itemizing your expenses, use this chart as a guide.

ESSENTIAL EXPENSES

Food $_____

Mortgage Payment/Rent $_____

Real Estate Taxes $_____

Utilities (gas, electric) $_____

Day Care $_____

Telephone $_____

Outstanding Loan Payments $_____

Charge Account Payments $_____

Insurance $_____

Medical/Dental $_____

Transportation $_____

Car (gas, oil, maintenance) $_____

Laundry/Dry Cleaning $_____

Other $_____
                                  $_____
                                  $_____
                                  $_____

Total $_____

NONESSENTIAL EXPENSES

Dining Out $_____

Clothing $_____

Entertainment $_____

Vacations $_____

Magazines, Books $_____

Manicures, Facials * $_____

    Hair Cuts/Coloring * $_____

    Miscellaneous $_____

    Total $_____

    (Essential + Nonessential Totals) $_____
    x No. of months estimated to new job = *Savings Goal*

* We've listed these as nonessentials (you can *survive* without them), but remember that it's important to look and feel great when interviewing. So do what you can yourself, then seek out a pro for the rest. For hair, begin with a good, professional cut—and do keep up the color.

Thus, if your income was $40,000 and your monthly expenses are $1,000, you need $4,000 in your Career Crisis Club. Bottom line? Over the course of three years, say, you should set aside about $110 per month.

Of course, this is the ideal. But given today's living costs, it may not be realistic. It also may not be totally necessary, since, at least if you're fired again, you'll probably be collecting unemployment benefits and, if you've played your cards right, a healthy severance. But don't let that be your excuse not to save. After all, you may not get enough severance or be eligible for unemployment. For instance, in many states, you have to be on a legal payroll for twenty-six weeks within a fifty-two-week period to qualify for unemployment.

Further, the amount of your severance may be minimal. Fair or not, a secretary probably will not be able to get the same consideration as a company vice president. (By the way, the best time to find out whether or not your company has a severance policy is while you're working. If there's no formal policy in place, try to discover how fired employees have been treated in the past. After all, you don't want any more surprises.)

Even if you're lucky and already have some savings stashed away, do continue to save, if not the full monthly amount, at least something each month, until you meet your goal. Then, DO NOT TOUCH THAT MONEY UNLESS AND UNTIL YOU ABSOLUTELY MUST.

(NOTE: A new Laura Ashley bedspread is *not* an absolute must, even if it *is* on sale.)

If, heaven forbid, your job search outlasts your unemployment checks, or some emergency arises—leave it to the air conditioner to die just as the thermometer hits 100°F—these extra savings will be a real lifesaver.

But there's another, nearly as important advantage to the Career Crisis Club: your peace of mind. Even with unemployment benefits coming in, women who've grown used to the self-sufficiency of a steady salary—and who too often live from paycheck to paycheck— panic when they lose their jobs. In nearly every WIN Workshop, someone brings up the fear—shared by nearly all the participants— that she'll wind up a bag lady walking the streets if she doesn't get a job fast!

Having a comfortable amount of savings neatly tucked away will lessen that fear and cushion the blow should the ax fall again. It will help keep you more calm and self-assured, which, in turn, will come across at your interviews and give you a better shot at that new job you want (and need). Desperation not only turns off prospective employers but also undermines, if not eliminates, your ability to negotiate.

What's more, your savings cushion will give you the confidence not to rush in and take the first job that comes along, but to wait for a position that you really want and can get excited about. Then, if you do get the job, and you have some money left over, you can use it to start your next Career Crisis Club. Or, you might want to take a little bit out and splurge on the beginnings of a new working wardrobe. Whatever the case, you'll be in better shape with some money in the bank.

Keeping an Updated Résumé

Résumés are important even *after* you've landed a job. Once you've settled in at your new company, can clearly describe your new responsibilities, and are feeling enthusiastic and optimistic, update your résumé. It's the ideal time.

Simply add the starting date and year of your current position (leave the closing date open-ended), and briefly describe your responsibilities. Then make at least twenty-five copies.

Here's where most people make a big mistake. They wait until they are desperate for a change or out of work to send their résumés to executive recruiters. But the best time to contact them is when you are happily employed. Think of it as another aspect of networking—letting people (in this case, placement people) know where you are and what you're up to.

Just mail the recruiters your résumé and enclose a short cover letter like this one:

Dear Al:
Thank you so much for the help you gave me in my recent job search. The interviewing tips you offered proved invaluable.

I love my new position, and feel I made the right choice.

I thought you might like to update your files, so I've enclosed my latest revised résumé. As you can see, I've included my new position and responsibilities here at Joffe Ltd.

Again, thanks so much for your help.

Sincerely,
Fay Sandler

Since it will probably take you a few months to adjust to your new spot, don't feel pressured to do this immediately, but try to do it within six months. After all, your company could be bought, the boss you love might quit and you'll hate his replacement (or worse yet, she'll hate you), the company may fall into dire financial straits, or your position may be eliminated.

Even if none of the above occurs and your job continues to challenge and excite you, you always have the option of saying no if a recruiter calls. But at least you'll get the call and have the option.

Researching Other
Companies and Careers

To paraphrase an old saying, the carpet's always plusher on the other side of the Xerox machine. Someone working in retail sales may think that magazine editors live a glamorous life. And those same magazine editors may believe that the really exciting jobs are on Wall Street.

Well, now that you're working and have the security and financial cushion of a paying job, you have an excellent opportunity to investigate another position, company, or field you think you'd like. You might have your eyes opened.

Here's what I mean. After being fired from her job as a copywriter, thirty-two-year-old Janet landed a spot with a small advertising agency. She'd actually wanted a position at a larger competitive firm in town but there were no openings at the time she needed work. She was at her job for about two months when she ran into an old friend whose wife happened to work at the larger agency. Janet called her and made a date for Sunday brunch, during which she got the lowdown on the much-desired firm: Everyone worked till at least 9:00 P.M. every night, last-minute weekend projects were common, the word "vacation" was not in the firm's vocabulary, all writers shared offices, and even though salaries were high, the company had an overworked revolving door.

Janet admits that without the objectivity and security of having a job, she might not have discovered this information or, if she had, might not have listened to it. Today, she has put pursuing her "dream company" aside and, while she happily plugs away at her job, she's researching two more firms for future possibilities.

Bear in mind that the more specific your objectives the easier and more productive your research will be. Knowing that you want "something to do with food" won't get you far. Instead, you need to decide specifically what you want to do with food. Write about it? Sell it? Be a recipe researcher for a magazine? Cater birthday parties for toddlers?

Thirty-year-old Rachel wanted to explore an entirely new field. A computer programmer by trade but a gourmet cook in her heart, she had always dreamed of working in a restaurant. When she was fired from her old firm—a company she'd worked for ever since college—the idea of starting a new career flitted by, but she was too panicked about money to give it much thought. Once she landed her new job, though, she decided to explore the food service business. Through friends of friends of friends (that's networking for you), she learned as much as she could—that she didn't like the business end, didn't want to work in a large restaurant where she'd have to start out peeling carrots all day, and, unfortunately, lacked the experience to snare the chef's spot at a small, established eatery.

In the process of doing her research, she met Christa and Daly, two women who wanted to open a small catering business in the heart of Greenwich Village. They had the financing and the business acumen, but needed an excellent cook who was ready to take a gamble with their new enterprise. They were impressed with Rachel and her culinary expertise and—voilá—asked her to join their venture. Six months later, they opened their doors. Rachel was—and still is—delighted! Clearly, researching does pay off.

Remember that when doing research you need as many specifics as possible. If you're investigating a similar job at another company, find out what your boss would be like and research salary levels, office conditions, attitudes about vacations, whether women have good promotional opportunities, and the company's financial stability and growth potential.

If you're researching a new field, find out whether the job market is already saturated or if there are lots of opportunities, what pay scales average, if it's a male bastion or if women can get ahead, if there are new skills you would have to learn, and whether you would be able to transfer your past experience fairly easily or have to begin at a low-paying entry level.

Corporate Graffiti:
The Handwriting on the Wall

Maybe you love your new job. And maybe it loves you. But nothing lasts forever, so this time be savvy and don't ignore the handwriting on the wall. It's the kind of corporate graffiti that demands your attention.

Often, many occurrences signal that a firing is coming, even though it's only in retrospect that most of us pay attention to them. (Of those women who answered our questionnaire, some 65 percent said they saw warnings but ignored them!) For example:

• A sportswear designer reports that her new boss starting relaying information directly to her staff, thus circumventing the normal line of communication, which would be to talk directly with her first.

• An assistant merchandiser remembers that she was given increasingly menial tasks. At one point she found herself with a bottle of Fantastik, cleaning the conference room table!

• An office manager recalls, now with a somewhat bitter laugh, that "they changed the locks six times when I worked there. The last time, they did not give me a new key."

• A vice president of marketing says she found herself excluded from several "closed-door meetings. I should have known something was up, but I convinced myself that I wasn't really needed at those meetings."

• One advertising creative director reports she was given "fewer and fewer assignments. Plus, I was passed over for promotion in favor of a younger man!"

• A regional sales manager says that "the president of the company was stalling on making decisions. For instance, he had told me to go ahead and hire an assistant. But every time I sent a good candidate on for his approval, he nitpicked, finding some obscure reason why he or she would not work out."

• A systems analyst says that her "co-workers became very quiet when I entered the room. Also, my usual lunchmates always seemed to be doing something else when noontime came."

244

Do any of these sound uncomfortably familiar? There are other signs you might be missing. For instance, you notice that other departments within the company are being "restructured"; be aware that yours might be, too. An interoffice memo from the president says the company is going on a new austerity plan; if you're in a high-salaried position, "possible cutbacks" may include your job. You are asked to train someone who is perfectly qualified to do your work; you may be training your replacement.

Perhaps the most common reason people get fired, though, is the arrival of new management. Often, new managers are told to "assess their staff" within three to six months and then make whatever changes they deem necessary. You may well be one of the changes.

Before you become completely paranoid, remember that in and of themselves, none of these "warnings" *necessarily* indicates that you're on your way out. Sometimes, closed-door meetings are only closed-door meetings. But do keep your antennae up. And certainly, if you begin to see a pattern forming, or several signs appear at once, take notice—and take action.

We've already talked about several of the ways you can and should protect yourself from an impending dismissal. But if the handwriting on the wall is getting bolder every day, there's another key precaution you should consider.

If your finances are low and you suspect your severance will be the same, go out and secure a small bank loan now. Get just enough to be able to make the necessary monthly payments and have something left to tide you over during your job search. Pat, whose working husband could help out, only needed $900; June, a single mother of two, got $9,000.

Remember, if you wait until you're fired, you are the last person your bank will want to see. If you don't get fired, you can pay the money back while you're working and the least you'll lose is the interest on the loan (which may be partially deductible anyway). So do it now!

Just one more thing. I cannot count how many people have told me, "I'm going to be fired on Friday," or next week, or whenever. If you're so sure a pink slip is due, rehearse your departing thoughts.

Practice what you may want to say and think about what you want to ask for. It will come in handy on firing day.

What to Do on Firing Day

Okay, it's happened again. But this time you have the opportunity to handle it a lot better, since, hopefully, you've negotiated severance going in and/or checked out the company's formal severance policy, stashed away some money in your Career Crisis Club, sent your résumé to recruiters, and networked, networked, networked. And experience has taught you that you *can* survive.

Still and all, "F-Day" is nerve-racking. So what's the best way to get through it? We've discussed several of the techniques in earlier chapters, but let's renew them, step by step.

(1) Stay calm. Remember you have some money in the bank, and more experience under your belt, so try not to panic.
(2) Don't get emotional. Hysterical outbursts in the office rarely serve any useful purpose, and they also prevent you from listening to what is being said.
(3) Find out exactly what kind of severance package (if any) you're being offered.
(4) After the boss has had his or her say, don't respond immediately, but ask to set up an appointment for exit negotiations.
(5) Don't sign anything until you've had time to think it through (or received professional advice).
(6) Re-read the chapter called "Negotiating Your Way Out" and follow its advice. Promise now. Don't just read it—DO IT!

Fortune Cookies Don't Lie

On the day of my last firing, my husband, trying to cheer me up, took me to my favorite Chinese restaurant for dinner. As if to mark the importance of the occasion, my cookie came with two fortunes. The first made me laugh. It said: "You love Chinese food."

The second made me stop and think. It said: "Now is the time to try something new."

It's been over three years since that eventful day, and now I know fortune cookies don't lie. It WAS the best time to try something new.

Getting fired pushed me out of a field I had outgrown and prompted me to start a business I love. It wasn't easy, and it was very scary, but at the same time it was—and is—exciting and extremely rewarding.

Now, the kind of business that I launched—running workshops for women who've been fired—may be unique. But let me assure you that what's happened to me is not. The overwhelming majority of women I've worked with who've lost their jobs have not only landed on their feet, but have moved on to better positions in their own industries or in new, more satisfying fields. Some have even started their own companies.

Does getting fired guarantee success? Of course not. But it does guarantee you the opportunity to reassess your passions, gather your resources, and go for it. So I'll say it one more time: Congratulations! Your best is yet to come.

BIBLIOGRAPHY
AND FURTHER RESOURCES

PSYCHOLOGICAL/STRATEGIC

Ciabattari, Jane. *Winning Moves: How to Come Out Ahead in a Corporate Shakeup.* New York: Rawson Associates, 1988.

Harragan, Betty Lehan. *Games Mother Never Taught You: Corporate Gamesmanship for Women.* New York: Warner Books, 1978.

Hyatt, Carole, and Gottlieb, Linda. *When Smart People Fail.* New York: Viking/Penguin, 1987.

Schenker, Susan. *Giving Away Success: How Women Get Stuck and What to Do About It.* New York: McGraw Hill, 1984.

Sher, Barbara, with Annie Gottlieb. *Wishcraft: How to Get What You Really Want.* New York: Ballantine Books, 1979.

Warschaw, Dr. Tessa Albert. *Rich Is Better: How Women Can Bridge the Gap Between Wanting and Having It All.* New York: Doubleday & Company, 1985.

JOB SEARCH

Crystal, John C., and Bolles, Richard N. *Where Do I Go from Here with My Life?* Berkeley, Calif.: Ten Speed Press, 1979.

German, Donald R., and German, Joan W. *How to Find a Job When Jobs Are Hard to Find.* New York: Amacom, 1981.

Snelling, Robert O. Sr. *The Right Job: How to Get the Job That's Right for You.* New York: Penguin Books, 1987.

Swain, Madeleine, and Swain, Robert S. *Out the Organization.* New York: MasterMedia Books, 1988.

RÉSUMÉS

Bostwick, Burdette E. *Résumé Writing: A Comprehensive How-to-Do-It Guide.* New York: John Wiley & Sons, 1985.

Jackson, Tom. *The Perfect Résumé.* New York: Doubleday & Company, 1981.

Levis, Adele. *How to Write Better Résumés.* 3d ed. New York: Barron's, 1989.

Schuman, Nancy, and Lewis, William. *Revising Your Résumé.* New York: John Wiley & Sons, 1987.

Smith, Michael Holley. *The Résumé Writer's Handbook.* New York: Barnes & Noble, 1987.

INTERVIEWING

Beatty, R. H. *The Five-Minute Interview.* New York: John Wiley & Sons, 1986.

Bell, Arthur H. *The Complete Manager's Guide to Interviewing: How to Hire the Best.* Irwin, Ill.: Dow Jones, 1989.

Krannich, Caryl Rae. *Interview for Success.* Manassas, Va.: Impact Publications, 1982.

Vlk, Suzee. *Interviews That Get Results.* New York: Simon & Schuster, 1984.

Yates, John Martin. *Knock 'Em Dead.* Holbrook, Mass.: Bob Adams, Inc., 1987.

NETWORKING

Cole, Diane. *Hunting the Headhunters: A Woman's Guide.* New York: Fireside, 1988.

Jackson, Tom. *The Hidden Job Market.* New York: Quadrangle, The New York Times Book Co., 1981.

Kleiman, Carol. *Women's Networks.* New York: Ballantine Books, 1982.

Krannich, Ronald L., and Krannich, Caryl Rae. *The Complete Guide to Networking Your Way to Job and Career Change*. Manassas, Va.: Impact Publications, 1988.

Welch, Mary Scott. *Networking—The Great New Way for Women to Get Ahead*. New York: Warner Books, 1980.

CAREER CHANGE

Bolles, Richard. *What Color Is Your Parachute? A Practical Manual for Job Hunters and Career-Changers*. Berkely, Calif.: Ten Speed Press, 1989.

Hyatt, Carole. *Shifting Gears: How to Master Career Change and Find the Work That's Right for You*. New York: Simon & Schuster, 1990.

Sinetar, Marsha. *Do What You Love: The Money Will Follow*. New York: Dell, 1989.

Viscott, David, M.D. *Risking*. New York: Simon & Schuster, 1977.

NEGOTIATING

Bachler, James R. *Book of Perks*. New York: St. Martin's Press, 1983. (Out of print)

Fisher, Roger, and Ury, William L. *Getting to Yes*. New York: Penguin, 1983.

Kennedy, Marilyn Moats. *Salary Negotiations*. New York: Scribners, 1982.

Nierenberg, Gerard. *The Art of Negotiating*. New York: Pocket Books, 1984.

Warschaw, Dr. Tessa Albert. *Winning by Negotiation*. New York: McGraw Hill, 1987.

STARTING YOUR OWN BUSINESS

Cohen, William A. *The Entrepreneur & Small Business Financial Problem Solver*. New York: John Wiley & Sons, 1989.

Fox, Philip J., and Mancuso, Joseph R. *402 Things You Must Know Before Starting a Business*. Englewood Cliffs, N.J.: Prentice Hall, 1980.

Greene, Gardiner G. *How to Start & Manage Your Own Business*. New York: Mentor, 1987.

Hisrich, Robert D., and Brush, Candida G. *The Woman Entrepreneur: Starting, Financing, and Managing a Successful New Business.* Lexington, Mass.: Lexington Books, 1986.

Mancuso, Joseph R. *How to Prepare & Present a Business Plan.* Englewood Cliffs, N.J.: Prentice Hall, 1983.

Scollard, Jeannette. *The Self-Employed Woman: How to Start Your Own Business and Gain Control of Your Life.* New York: Simon & Schuster, 1985.

Wilkens, Joanne. *Her Own Business: Successful Secrets of Entrepreneurial Women.* New York: McGraw Hill, 1988.

West, Alan. *A Business Plan (Planning for the Small Business).* London: Nichols, 1988.

GENERAL REFERENCE/MISCELLANEOUS

Bacon's Publicity Checker. Chicago: Bacon's PR & Media Information Systems, 1990.

Directories in Print (Parts I & II). Detroit: Gale Research, Inc., 1989.

Encyclopedia of Associations. Detroit: Gale Research, Inc., 1989.

Rapoport, John D., and Zevnik, Brian L.P. *The Employee Strikes Back! What You Must Know About Sexual Harassment, Age Discrimination, Drug Testing, Polygraph Abuse, Unfair Performance Appraisals, Wrongful Firing and More.* New York: Macmillan, 1989.

Readers' Guide to Periodical Literature. (Check your local library.)

Todd, Alden. *Finding Facts Fast: How to Find Out What You Want to Know Immediately.* New York: William Morrow, 1979.

Zeitz, Baila, Ph.D., and Dusty, Lorraine. *The Best Companies for Women.* New York: Simon & Schuster, 1988.

HELPFUL ORGANIZATIONS

AWED (American Women's Economic Development Corp.)
60 East 42nd Street
Suite 405
New York, NY 10165
1-800-222-AWED

Catalyst
14 East 60th Street
New York, NY 10022
212-759-9700

NAFE (National Association for Female Executives)
127 West 24th Street
New York, NY 10011
212-645-0770

NAWBO (National Association of Women Business Owners)
600 South Federal Street
Suite 400
Chicago, IL 60605
312-922-0465

National Small Business Administration
1604 K Street, N.W.
Washington, D.C. 20006
The Answer Desk: 1-800-368-5855

INDEX